Wisdom With Understanding is Better Than Rubies

Lurine Karon Greenberg
Fine Arts Collection

OCCUPIED JAPAN

COLLECTIBLES

Identification & Value Guide

GENE
FLORENCE

COLLECTOR BOOKS
A Division of Schroeder Publishing Co., Inc.

The current values in this book should be used only as a guide. They are not intended to set prices, which vary from one section of the country to another. Auction prices as well as dealer prices vary greatly and are affected by condition as well as demand. Neither the author nor the publisher assumes responsibility for any losses that might be incurred as a result of consulting this guide.

Cover design by Beth Summers
Book design by Beth Ray

Searching For A Publisher?

We are always looking for people knowledgeable within their fields. If you feel that there is a real need for a book on your collectible subject and have a large comprehensive collection, contact Collector Books.

COLLECTOR BOOKS
P.O. Box 3009
Paducah, Kentucky 42002-3009
www.collectorbooks.com

Copyright © 2001 by Gene Florence

～ Contents ～

~ Foreword ~

"Made in Occupied Japan" has been an intriguing phrase for collectors over the years, but as many new collectors join this collecting society, the quantity of pieces so marked has declined exponentially! In the nine years since my Fifth book, there have been many changes in collecting fields. National newspapers and magazines have carried columns about this collecting domain. With the advent of the Internet and a multitude of television shows dedicated to informing (or misinforming) the public on collectibles, recognition of OJ has been achieved for many people who had no idea that there were collectors looking for items marked in this way. You should realize that often the few pieces of Occupied Japan items shown on TV shows are greatly over valued. Don't take all the values given on TV as gospel since to help sensationalize their shows, upper end valuations are almost always espoused. (For example, an Occupied Japan sewing machine shown recently that would have a hard time fetching $125.00, was appraised as worth hundreds of dollars.)

For those readers who have not seen my previous editions, I restate some basic information.

All items made in Japan from the beginning of our occupation at the end of World War II until April 28, 1952, when the occupation ended, that were to be exported to the United States had to be marked in one of four ways: "Japan," "Made in Occupied Japan," "Occupied Japan," or "Made in Japan." You can see that if all the markings were used proportionately or nearly so, then only about half of the items imported into the United States would have been marked with the magic words for collectors, "Made in OCCUPIED JAPAN." Thus, you will find that there are many similar or like items that will be marked only "Japan" or "Made in Japan."

There is no way of substantiating that these were actually made in Occupied Japan. (For the sake of brevity, capital letters "MIOJ" and "OJ" are used throughout the collecting world to mean "Made in Occupied Japan" or "Occupied Japan.") I must emphasize, unless an item actually says "Occupied" in some form, it will not be considered to be such. There is one exception to that rule, and that applies to items found in original containers such as boxes or car-

tons where the container is marked "MIOJ" while the items within are only marked "Japan." However, these items must always stay with the original container to be certified as "Occupied." From past observation and correspondence with collectors over the years, it is obvious that a large number of items imported from Japan during this time were marked on the containers only, and, of course, many of these original containers have been discarded. The items were marked to satisfy governmental policies. The original consumers did not care whether or not an item was marked "OJ." It is speculated that only a small percentage of the larger, finer wares were themselves marked "MIOJ." Today, the dearth of these larger marked pieces makes them prized by collectors as very desirable to own. If you have a choice between buying one quality piece or several smaller items, I recommend you consider buying the one distinctive piece.

All items photographed in this book are marked OJ or MIOJ in some form unless noted. Many times only the box or one item in a set will be marked. In the case of salt and pepper sets, the shakers will be sitting on something marked MIOJ, but the shakers themselves may not be marked MIOJ.

There are a multitude of markings and colors for Occupied Japan pieces. Most commonly found is black, but, in my experience, other colored marks do not detract or enhance values themselves, though I realize at least one author disagrees with me on this.

Measurements to the nearest eighth of an inch are given for several pieces on each page, and if needed, additional measurements have been added. This should help you in pricing similar pieces of OJ. There are many OJ pieces, especially figurines, that can be found in several sizes. In most cases, bigger is better; however, quality of the item is the major determining factor!

Be aware that there are counterfeits and reproductions available. Buy from reputable dealers if you are spending large amounts of your hard-earned money. If an item is glazed on the bottom, the mark will be under the glaze and not on top of it! After a while, experience will enable you to spot an Occupied Japan piece before you even turn it over to look for the mark.

There is an Occupied Japan Collectors Club on the East Coast which has an annual Occupied Japan show! You can get additional information by sending an SASE to: O.J. Club c/o Florence Archambalt, 29 Freeborn Street, Dept GF, Newport, RI 02840. Dues are $20.00 yearly, and there is a monthly newsletter to keep you up to date.

~ Acknowledgments ~

Sadly, as I sat down to write this, I realized that this is the first Occupied Japan book that I have done since the death of my mom who was known as "Grannie Bear" to all our customers. I acknowledge that we miss her still and all her help sorting and arranging various pieces into categories. It was a task she always insisted was her "part" in getting books published for collectors' use, and she was very much a part of the previous five books. In truth, her voice was echoing, "When are you going to photograph those new OJ pieces for another book, boy?" which, doubtless, prompted this one.

I wish to pay a special thanks to my family for pitching in and helping make this book possible. Over the years, they have done whatever has been needed. Cathy, my wife, unwrapped, carefully recorded markings, and measured the pieces for each new photo-

graph before wrapping the items again, a labor intensive, time consuming project. The boys, though out on their own, helped with loading and unloading and did various computer perks. In-laws, Charles and Sibyl, helped with sorting, packing, and taking care of our domicile while we were traveling and photographing.

Charles Lynch and Richard Walker did all the additional photography needed and worked tirelessly on the cover shot. Jane White and Zibby Walker aptly aided us at the studio, arranging the variety of items into some semblance of order. Beth Ray collated the various photographs and text into page layouts. A book is never one person's work. It's a grand team effort, and we had an excellent team working on this. We hope you enjoy our efforts to bring you this little peek into the vast world of Occupied Japan items.

~ Introduction ~

Per the publisher's request, this book is a choice compilation of my previous five books with additional items never shown in any of those books. We tried in this sixth book to cover a wide range of items being seen in the market place. From my first book published in 1976 to the fifth in 1992, there has been a vast change in the collecting of Occupied Japan. There were relatively few knowledgeable collectors around during the first edition, but by 1992, there were thousands. Now, in the new millennium, the expanding information about Occupied Japan collectibles has mushroomed across international boundaries with the introduction of the Internet into our lives. Few people owned computers in 1992; today, few people do not have access to one, even if the local library owns it! Not only has the Internet opened up information about collectibles, it has provided auctions where collectibles can change hands. This is good for collectors in that they have access to items they may never have seen before or otherwise had the opportunity to own. They can often find good bargains and fairly priced merchandise. The down side is that (as with any auction) prices can "get out of hand" quickly if two or more people are determined to own the same item! While this may be a dream come true for one seller, it may set an artificially high ceiling for the rest of the market, which ultimately discourages regular commerce for future buyers and sellers alike. Don't be led into believing ONE auction price is THE price of an item. It was the price for that moment, under those circumstances. You could just as easily find a like item two weeks later selling for half that amount. As an author, though noting auction and dealer advertised prices, I view these with a somewhat jaundiced eye. Rather, I try to find out actual selling prices of items; and thankfully, I know dealers who are willing to share that information with me. You have thousands of pieces priced in this book; hopefully, from this information you will be able to ascertain the pricing realm for items you own.

~ Pricing ~

All prices in this book are retail. The last thing I do for any book is to go over the prices, updating any new developments that may occur after the writing is finished. This is not as critical in OJ as in other fields of collecting, but with publishing lead times as they are today, I want you to know that the prices are current. The Internet auctions have changed both collecting habits and pricing considerations. I used to sell thousands of pieces of MIOJ in my shop each year; but after Mom's death, I closed the shop. I now sell Occupied Japan through a booth in an antique mall and on the Internet. You can find my web page at www.geneflorence.com and my auctions on eBay under dgfk19. I only mention this to let you know that the prices listed are not "hoped-for" prices, but actual selling prices.

You will see higher and lower prices for OJ than are listed in this book. I say that for the lady from the West who admonished me at length because I priced OJ way too cheaply, and for the man in the East, who wrote to say I priced OJ so high that nobody in the world could get those prices out of it.

Yard and garage sales as well as auctions are good sources for finding bargains on OJ, but more and more people are becoming aware of THE MARK, MIOJ. Be ready to pay a fair price and count on finding a bargain or two. You will see some inflated prices time and again. Unfortunately, people with a little bit of knowledge about MIOJ sometimes think that Occupied Japan is a gold mine – especially if they are the one who owns it.

This book is meant as a guide only. Only the buyer and the seller can determine actual worth ... what one is willing to sell for and what one is willing to pay. That is the price no matter what the book says! I buy and sell. I have to make those decisions often.

Many times I leave pieces I would love to own but believe the price is out of line. You have to determine your limits as a collector or as a dealer. I reiterate, these prices are meant to be a good, general guide.

Prices are listed as retail; thus, if you want to sell some of your collection to a dealer, you will have to discount them. Most dealers are willing to pay 50% to 60% of the retail price of sought items. Common or hard to sell items will have to be discounted much more. Remember, the better quality of the piece or the more unusual it is, the more collectors will be looking for it.

Collectors look for mint items. The prices listed in this book are for mint condition items. That means having all the parts; no cracks, chips or glued pieces are acceptable as mint. Unless it is very unusual and hard to find, there is little value to a damaged piece.

As in the previous five books, I have included a price range for each piece. Several collectors have told me, "I buy at low book and sell at high." Be your own judge. It is your money and only you can determine how you spend it.

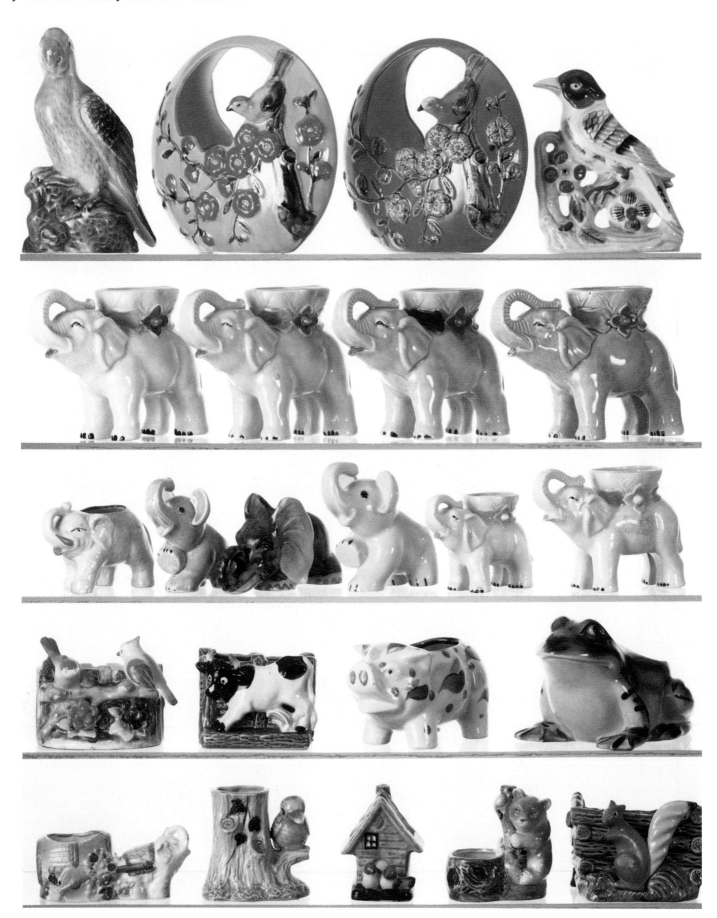

Animals and Animal Planters

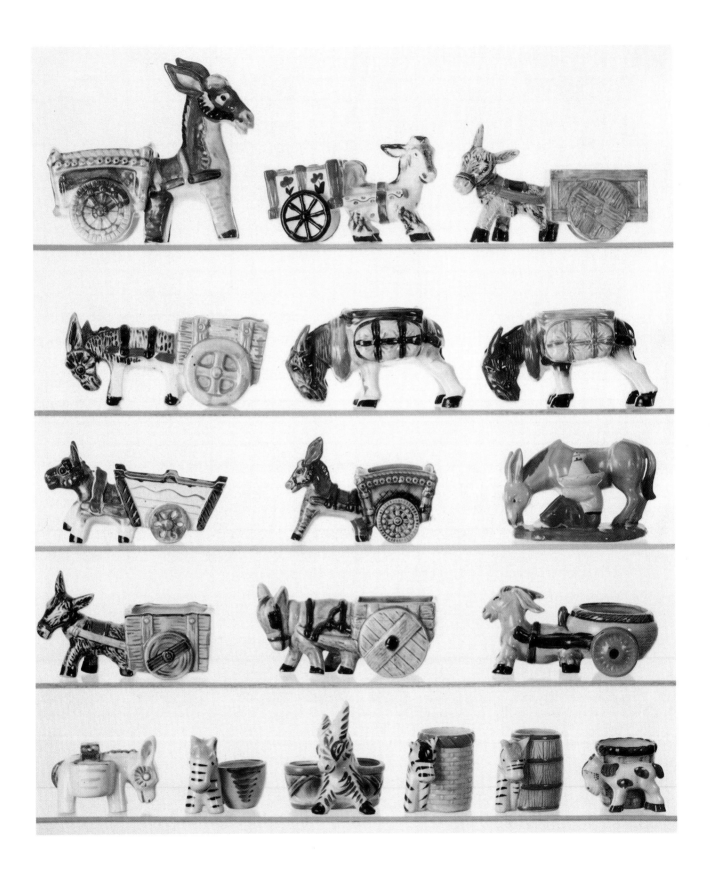

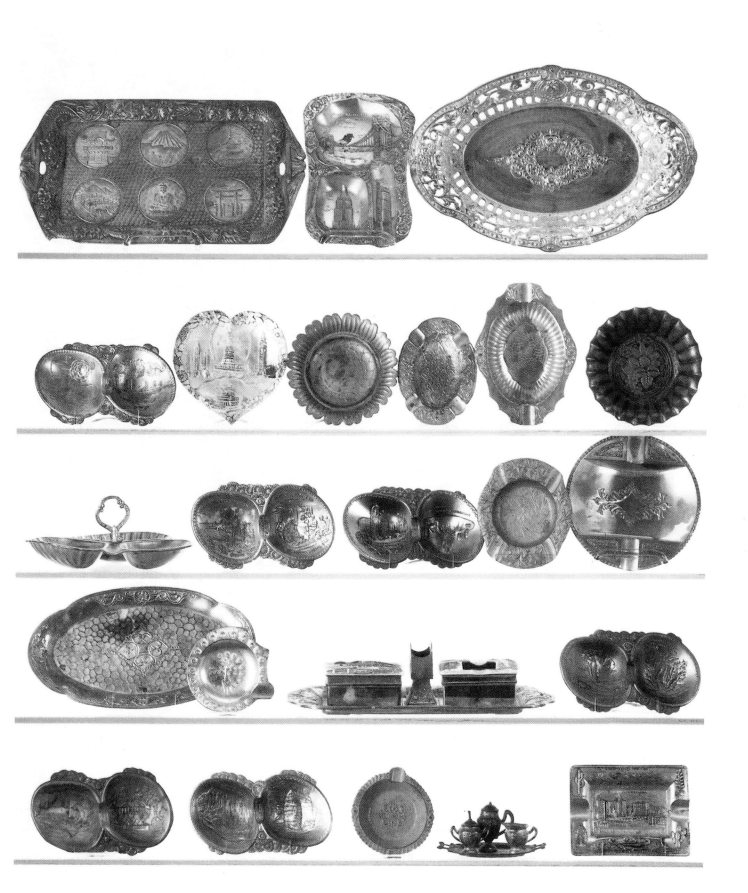

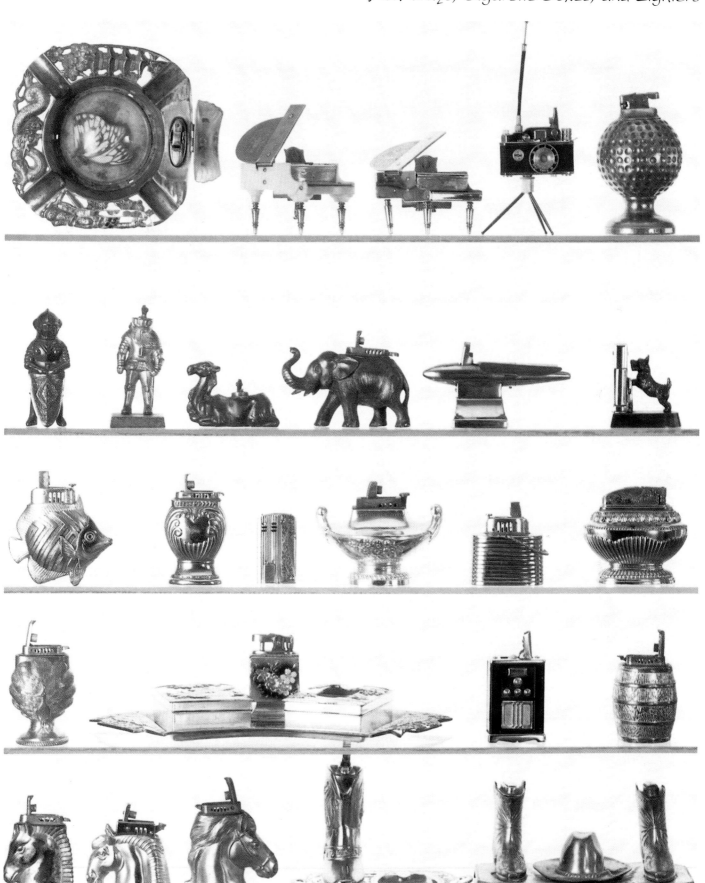

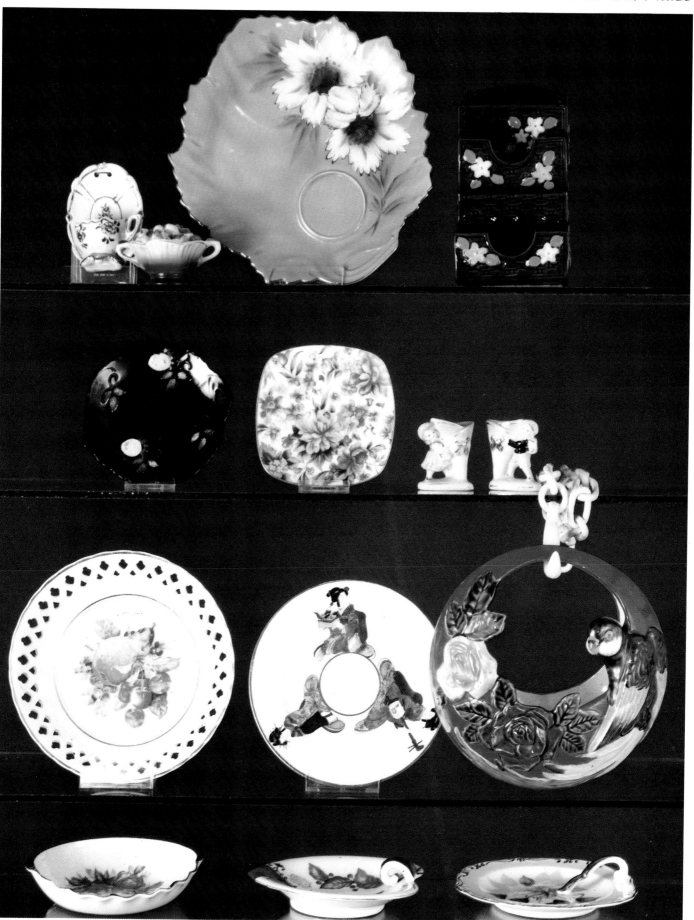

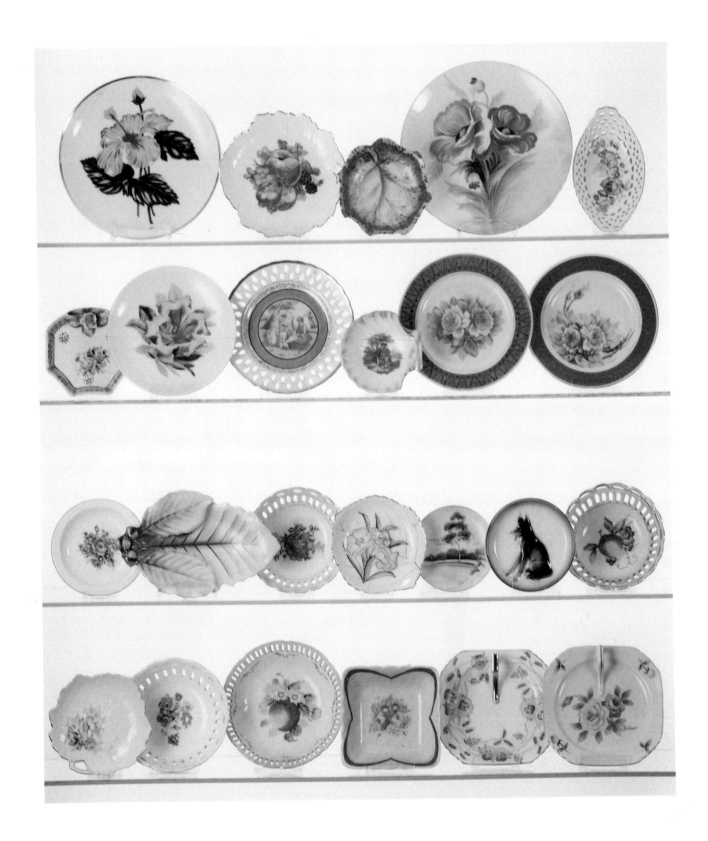

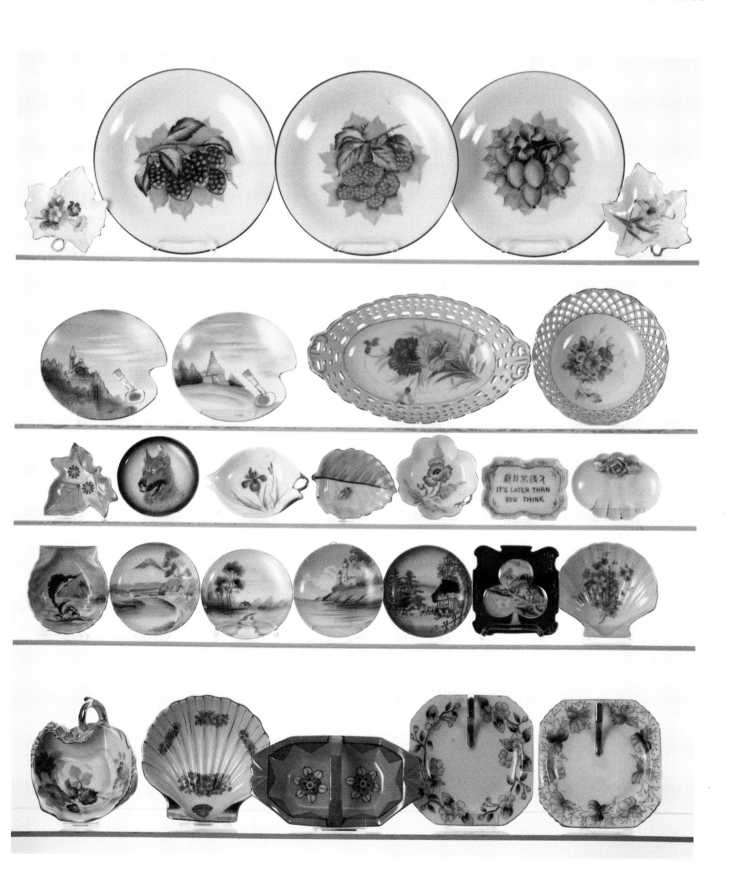

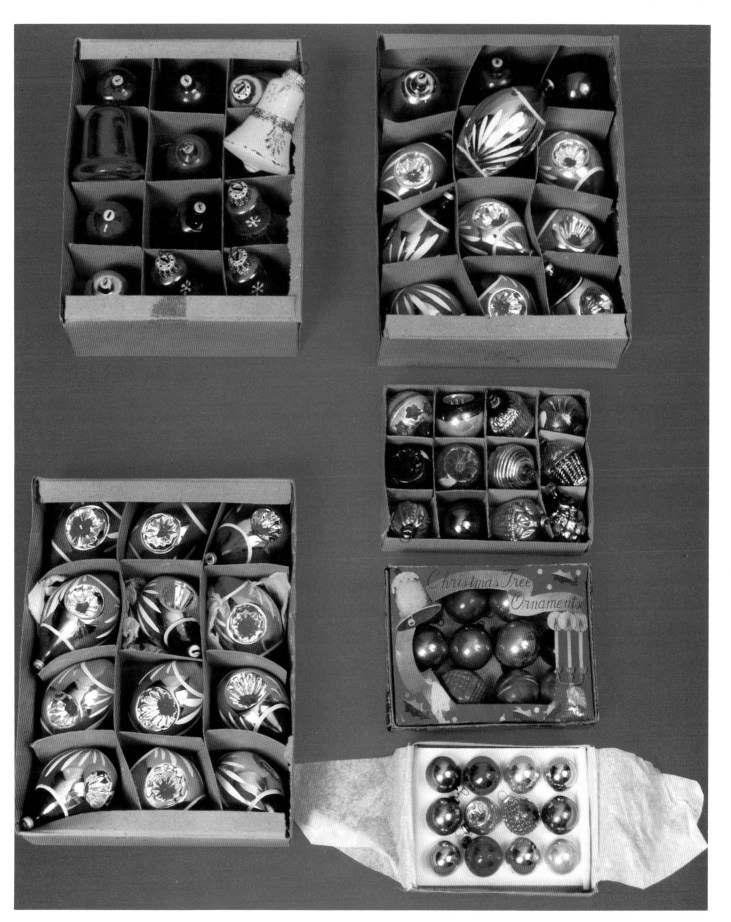

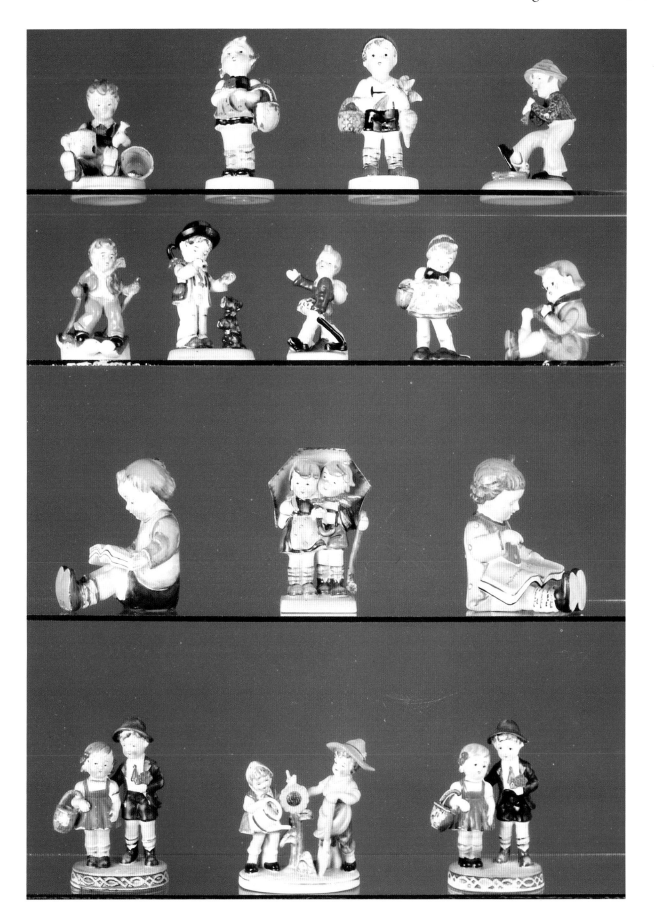

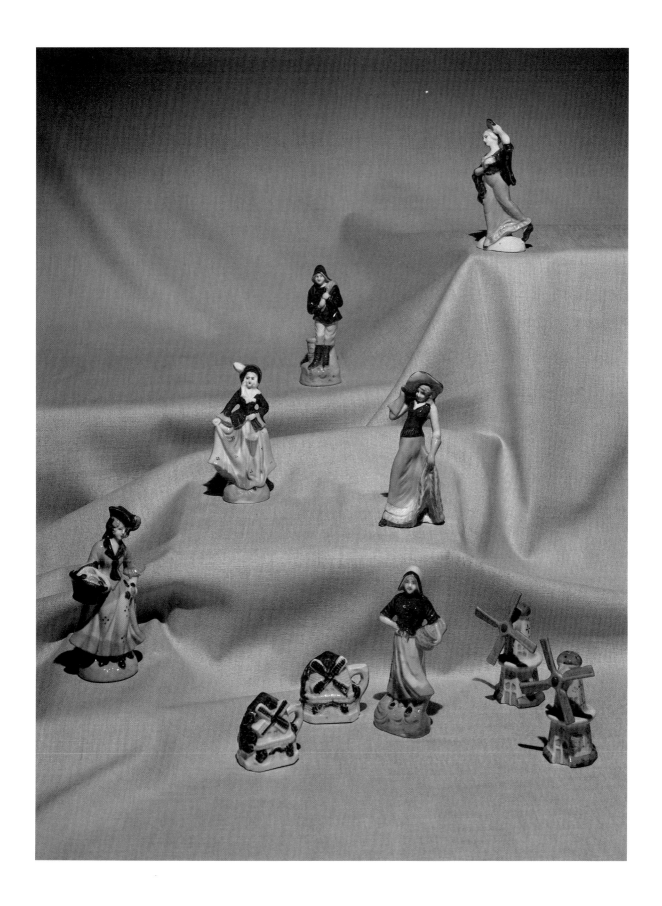

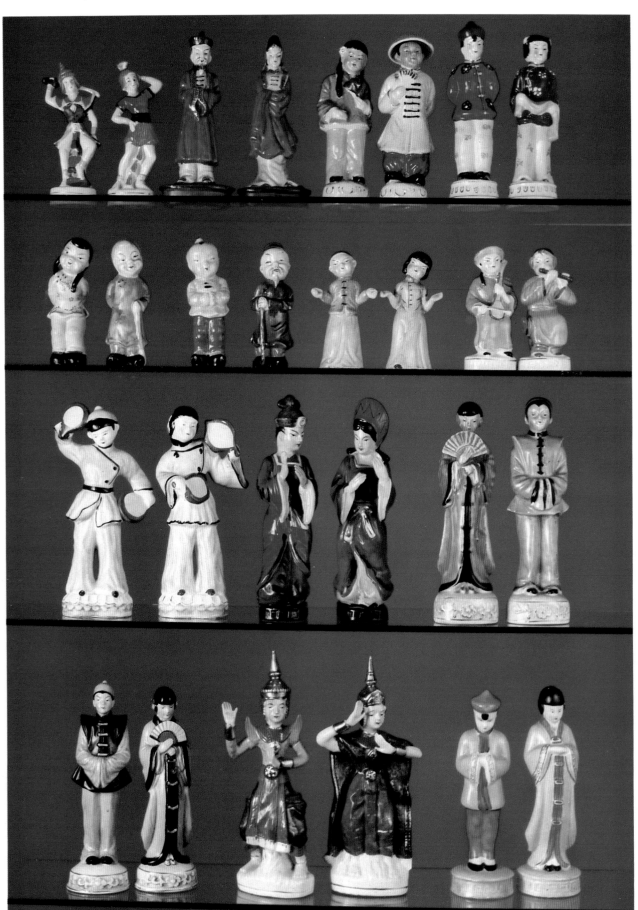

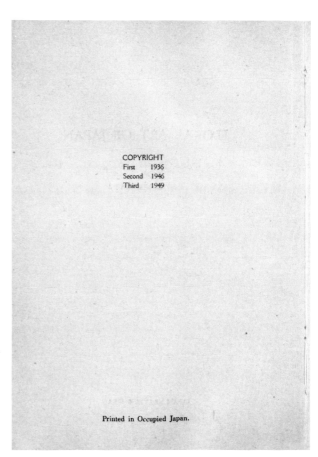

COPYRIGHT
First   1936
Second   1946
Third   1949

Printed in Occupied Japan.

Arranged by Mrs. Riei Ikeda

This novel, though artistic group is an example of
the sanjuike (triple arrangement)

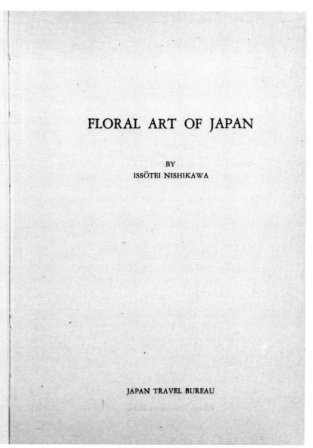

FLORAL ART OF JAPAN

BY
ISSŌTEI NISHIKAWA

JAPAN TRAVEL BUREAU

The Army and Navy
Needle Book
Contains a full variety of
Large Eyed Needles

The Holiday
Needle Assortment

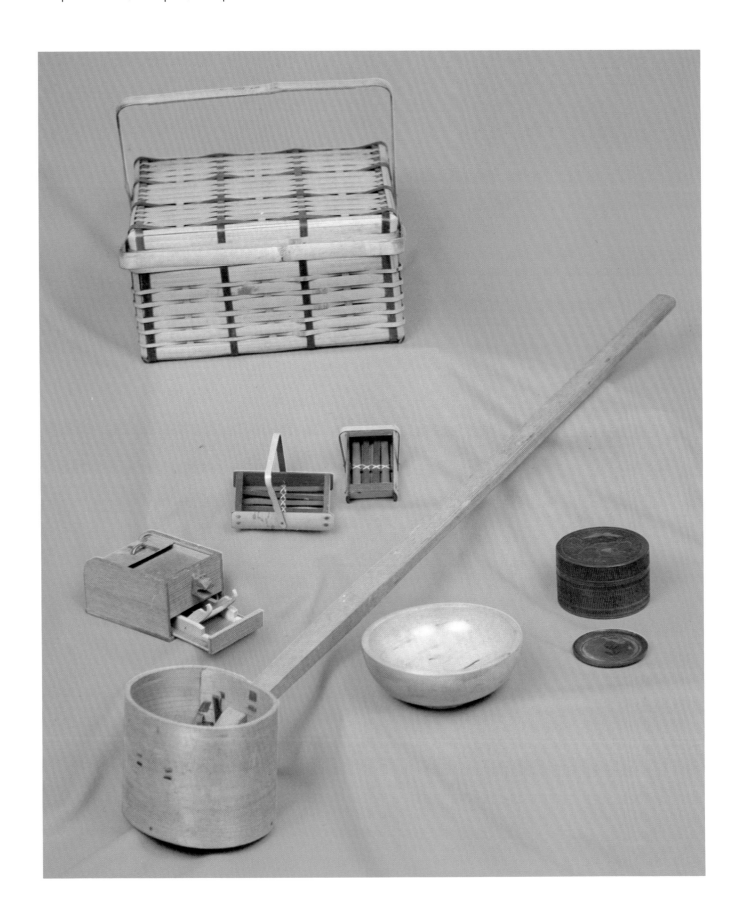

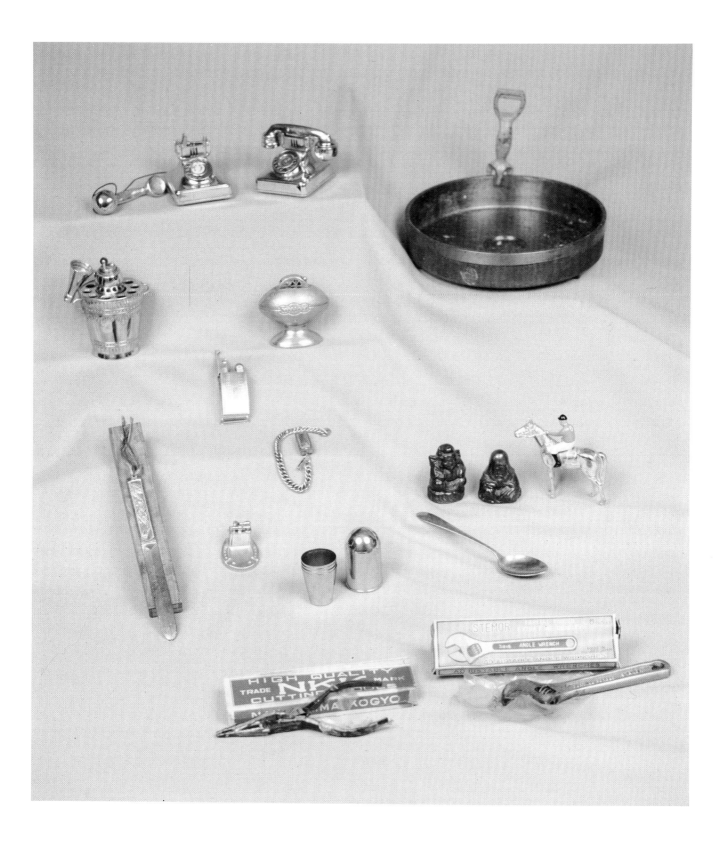

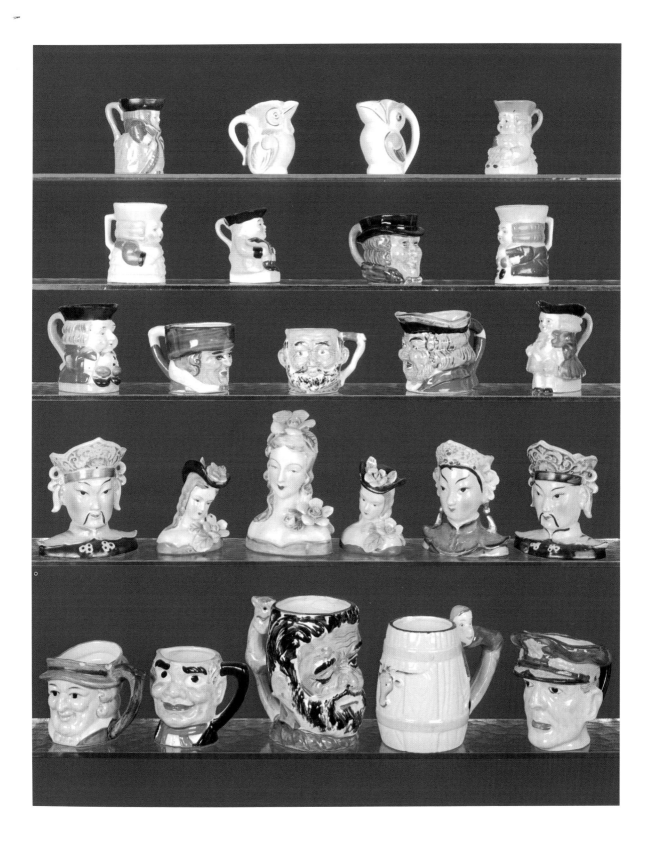

~ Salt and Pepper Shakers ~

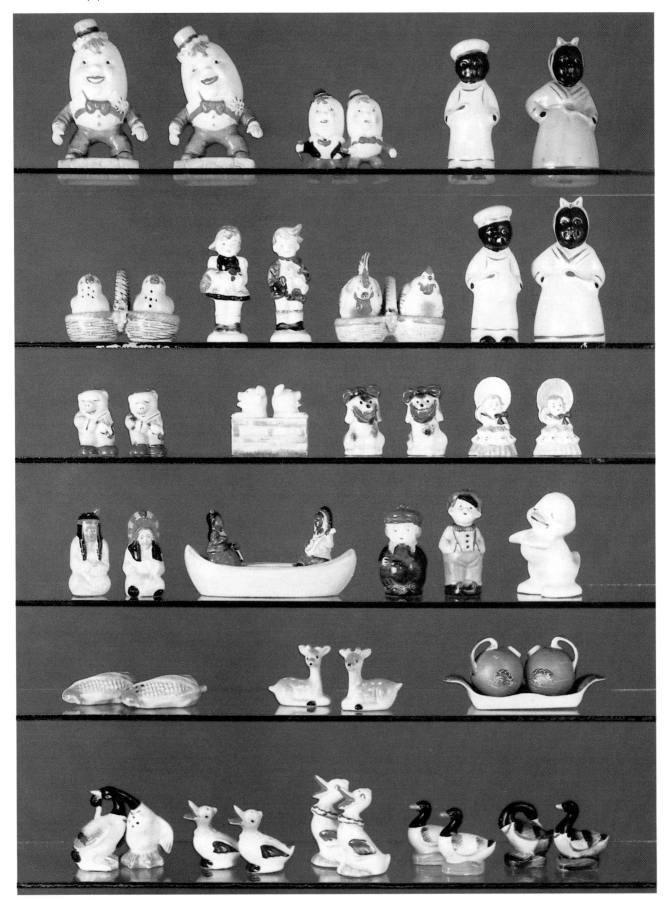

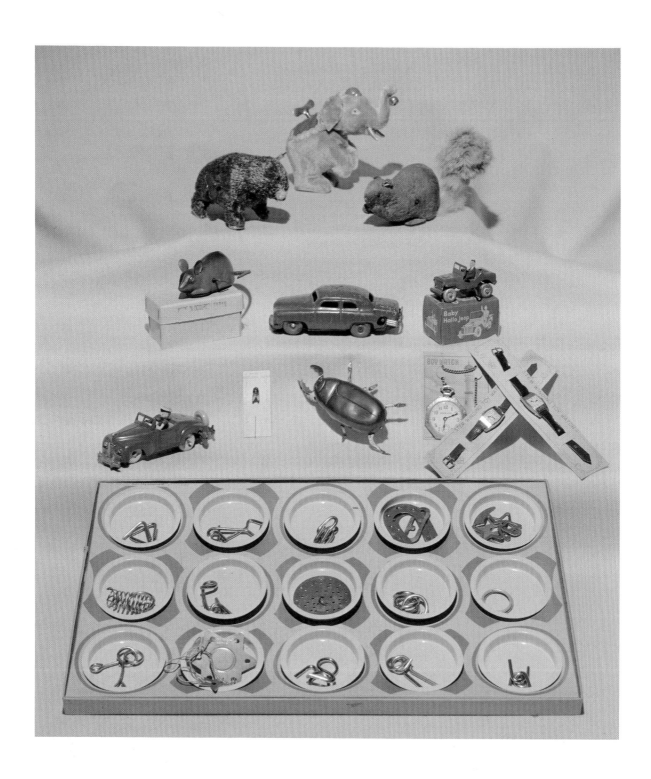

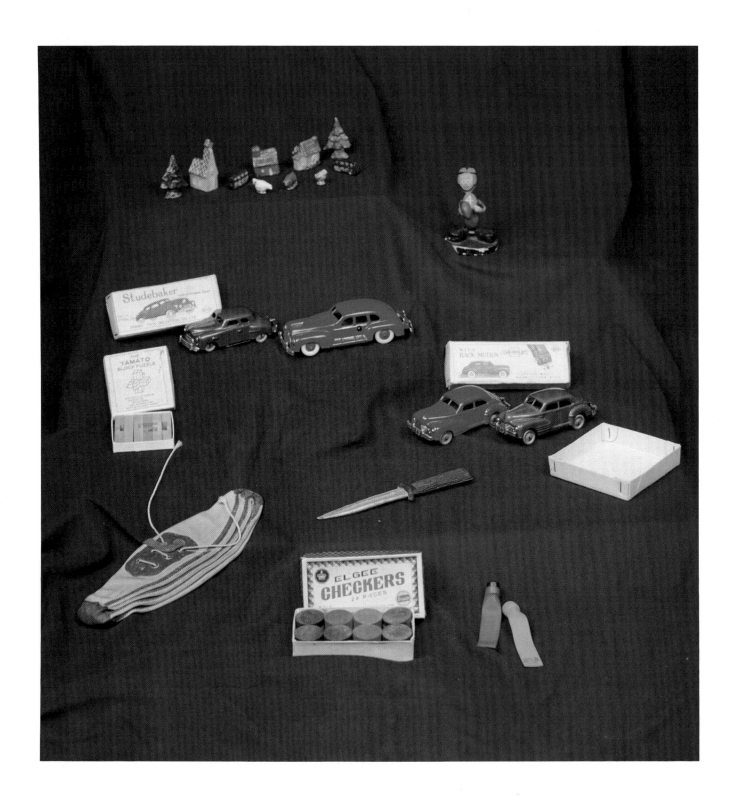

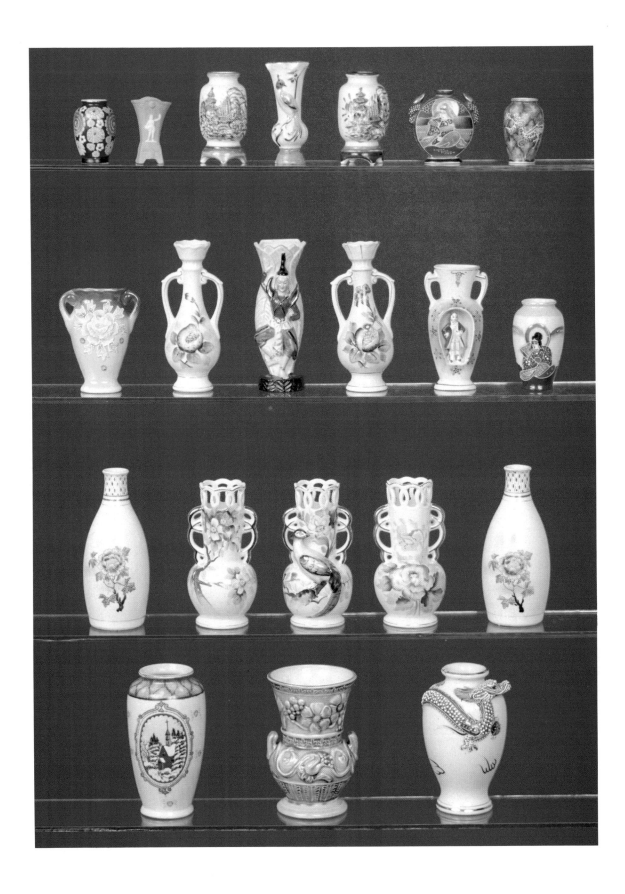

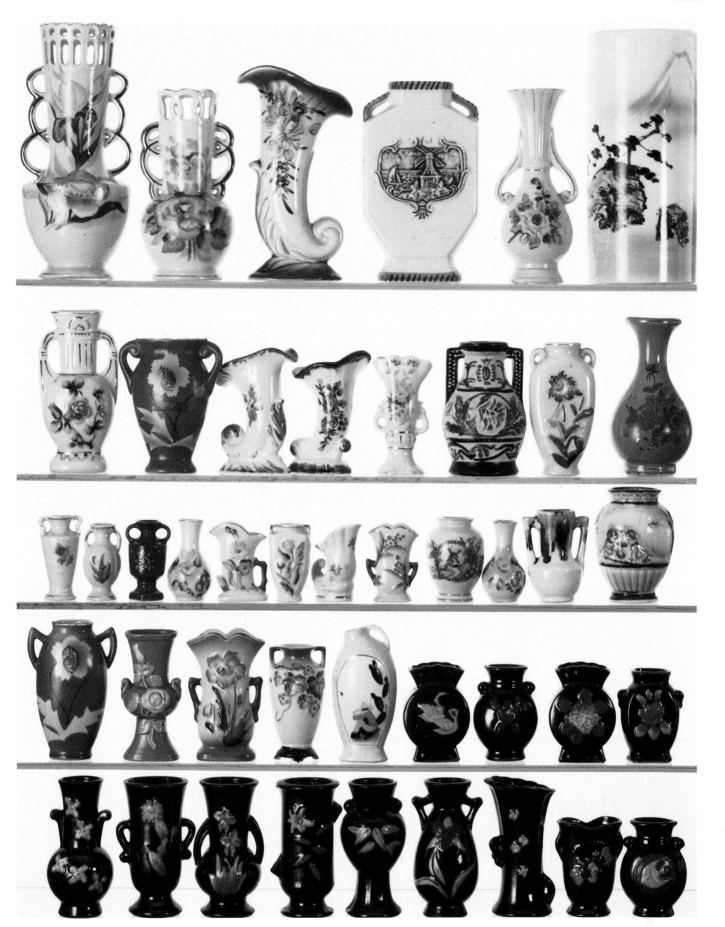

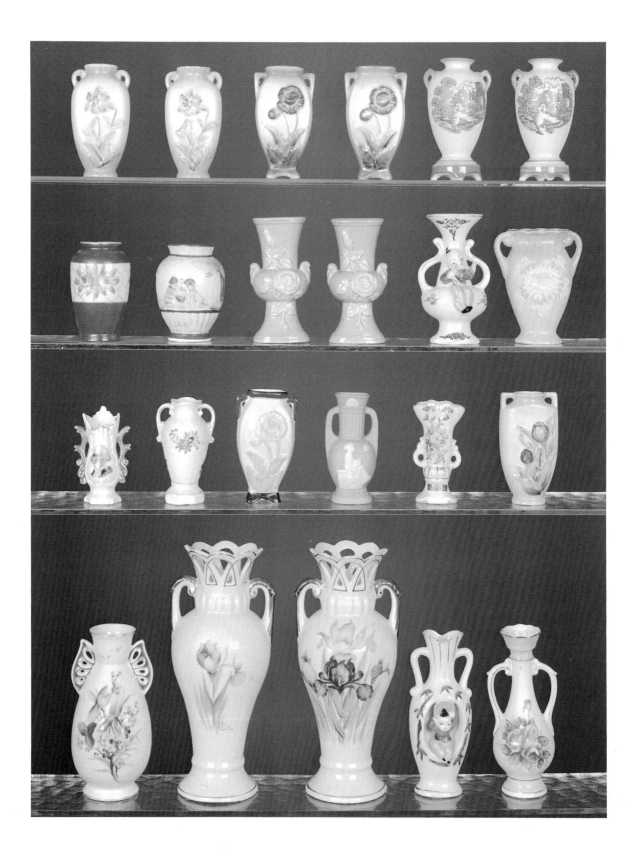

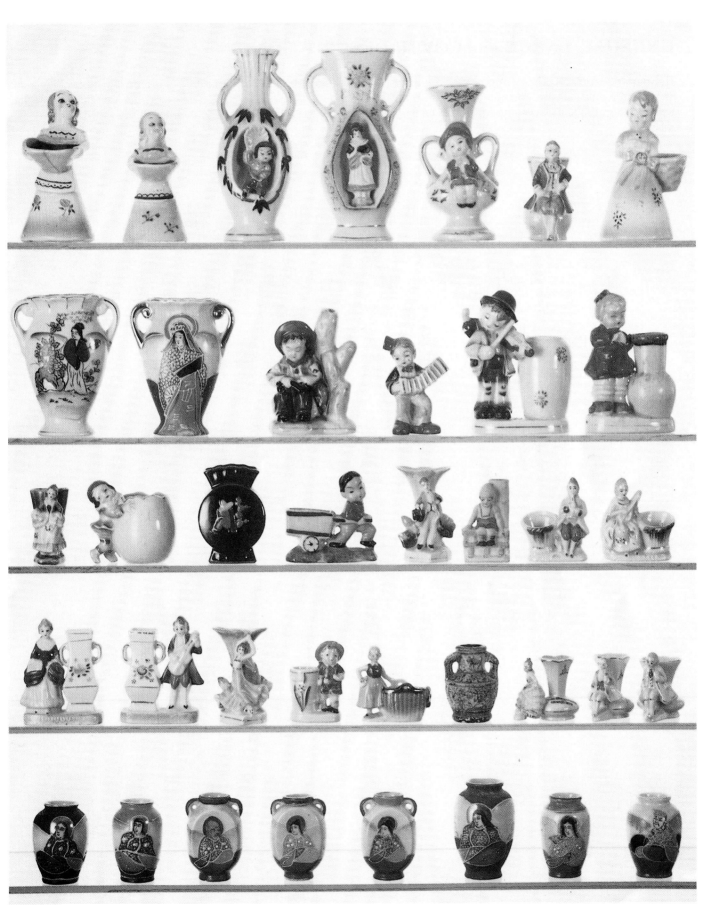

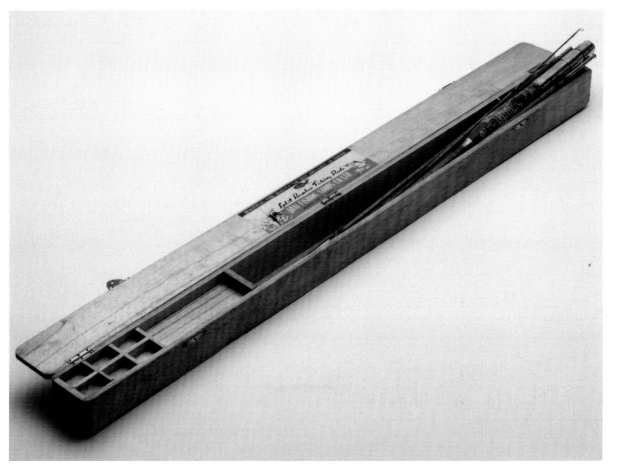

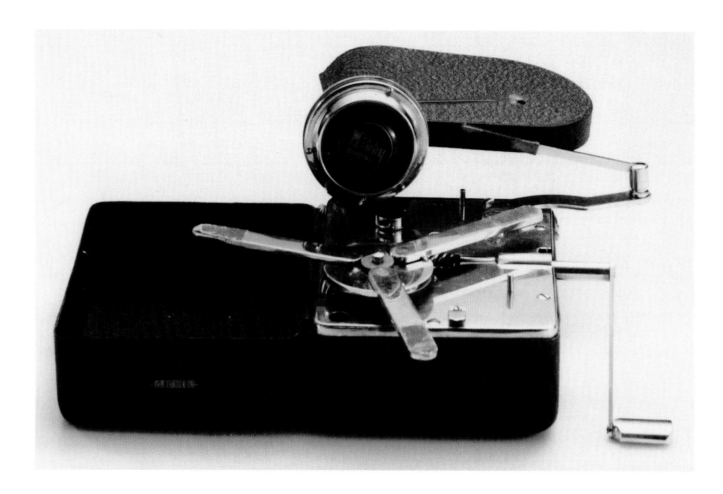

1) Place machine on table with Mikky phone sign up.
2) Push silver button on right side.
3) In left cover remove speaker — fits tight.
4) Remove hand crank at base of machine on right side.
5) Turn three-fingered dial to clear on side and tighten down center screw.
6) Remove Mikky (sic) phone by pulling up.
7) On the right side push up to the top of the machine, a 180° turn the folded metal arm.
8) Open the three fingers, to the stops.
9) Take the metal speaker, place so opening is down and attach needle part. Has semi-lock on it.
10) Raise small arm up and slide speaker onto it.
11) Crank goes into side and turn it. Please do not wind tight.
12) Place record on the 3-fingers.
13) Pull needle arm down 90° until it is over the button that you used to open the machine.
14) Record is now turning. Place needle on record.
15) Should be all set.

~ Price Guide ~

Page 6

Top Row:
1st, Cherub, 5¾" ....$30.00 – 35.00
2nd and 5th, Cherubs ....$30.00 – 35.00 ea.
3rd and 4th, Angels Playing Tambourine,
 7¼" ....$70.00 – 85.00 ea.

2nd Row:
Angel on Pink Basket, 5" ..$55.00 – 60.00
Angel with Shell on Back,
 5⅛" ....$50.00 – 55.00
Angel Sitting on Cornucopia .$55.00 – 65.00
Angel w/Donkey, 4⅛" ....$25.00 – 30.00

3rd Row:
Cherub Holding Bowl, 5½".$55.00 – 65.00
Angel Fixing Halo ....$50.00 – 60.00
Angel at Anvil ....$50.00 – 60.00
Angel w/Donkey ....$50.00 – 60.00

4th Row:
Cherub Vase, 3⅜" ....$12.50 – 15.00
Angel w/Shell ....$50.00 – 55.00
Angel w/Wheelbarrow ......$30.00 – 35.00
4th and 5th Angel Bud Vases,
 5¼" ....$20.00 – 25.00 ea.

5th Row:
1st, Angel Planter ....$30.00 – 35.00
2nd and 4th, Angels on
 Butterfly.......................$25.00 – 30.00 ea.
3rd, Powder Box............$90.00 – 100.00
5th, Angel w/Shell ....$30.00 – 35.00

Page 7

Top Row:
Cherub, 5" ....$12.50 – 15.00
Cherub, 3⅝" ....$8.00 – 10.00
Angel w/Mandolin, 6⅜"....$25.00 – 30.00
Cherub w/Horn, 6⅝" ....$30.00 – 35.00
Angel Pair, 6" ....$35.00 – 40.00

2nd Row:
1st, 3rd, 4th Angels............$8.00 – 10.00 ea.
2nd, Cherub, pair ....$20.00 – 25.00
5th, Angel w/Lattice Basket .$25.00 – 30.00

3rd Row:
Angel w/Mandolin, 2⅝".........$4.00 – 5.00
Angel w/Drum..................$10.00 – 12.00
Cherub, pair w/grapes .....$25.00 – 30.00
4th, 5th, 6th, Angel Vases,
 4" ....$12.00 – 15.00 ea.

4th Row:
1st – 7th, Angel Vases, 4" .$12.00 – 15.00 ea.

5th Row:
1st – 4th, Angels, 2⅛" ....$5.00 – 6.00 ea.
5th – 7th, Angels, 3" ....$10.00 – 12.00 ea.
8th, Angel, 2½" ....$7.50 – 9.00

Page 8

Top Row:
1st and 3rd Flower Cupids,
 4" ....$30.00 – 35.00 ea.

2nd Cupid w/Flower Snail,
 4½" x 6" ....$35.00 – 40.00

2nd Row:
1st and 6th Cupid on Sled,
 5" ....$40.00 – 45.00 ea.
2nd, 3rd, 4th, and 5th Musicians,
 3¼" ....$8.00 – 10.00 ea.

3rd Row:
1st Butterfly Babe, 3¼" .....$25.00 – 30.00
2nd, 3rd, 4th, and 5th Angels, 2" to
 2½" ....$7.50 – 9.00 ea.
6th, 7th, 8th, and 9th Musician,
 2½" ....$5.00 – 6.00 ea.

4th Row:
1st and 6th Angel Vases,
 7½" ....$55.00 – 60.00 ea.
2nd Candleholder, 6" ....$45.00 – 50.00
3rd Angel Drummer, 5¼" ..$30.00 – 35.00
4th Angel w/Horn, 5" ....$25.00 – 30.00
5th Arrow Repair Cupid, 7"..$40.00 – 45.00

5th Row:
1st Cupid w/Donkey, 4".....$25.00 – 30.00
2nd Nude on Seahorse, 3½" .$17.50 – 20.00
3rd Angel Planter, 3½" .....$15.00 – 17.50
4th and 5th Cupid w/Moon,
 3½" ....$8.00 – 10.00 ea.
6th and 7th Angel Bud Vase,
 2¾" ....$10.00 – 12.00 ea.

Page 9

Top Row:
Cow, 2¾" x 4" ....$8.00 – 10.00
Elsie, 3½" ....$17.50 – 20.00
Squirrels, 4½" x 5" ....$17.50 – 20.00
Pig, 2½" x 3½" ....$10.00 – 12.50
Cow set, large 2¾" x 4", small
 1¼" ....$20.00 – 22.50

2nd Row:
Horse, 2¼" ....$4.00 – 5.00
Cat, 2" ....$4.00 – 5.00
Cats, 1¼" ....$6.00 – 7.50
Dogs, 2¼" ....$8.00 – 10.00
Dogs, terriers, 3½" ....$15.00 – 17.50
Scotties, three white or black ..$8.00 – 10.00
Dogs in Basket, 3¼".........$12.50 – 15.00
Dog, blue, 1¾" x 3¼" ....$6.00 – 7.50
Dog, 3¾" ....$12.50 – 15.00

3rd Row:
Dog w/Lamp, 2" ....$3.00 – 4.00
Dog, begging, 2½" ....$4.00 – 5.00
Dog w/Pups, 2⅛" ....$7.00 – 7.50
Poodle, 3" ....$12.50 – 15.00
Shepherd, 1¾" x 3¼" ....$5.00 – 6.00
Dog, green, 2" x 3" ....$5.00 – 6.00
Dog, pair, 2" ....$7.50 – 10.00
Dog w/Horn, 3½" ....$7.00 – 8.50
Puppies, 2" ....$4.00 – 5.00

4th Row:
Dog, 4½" x 5½" ....$15.00 – 17.50
Dog, 5½" x 7" ....$15.00 – 17.50
Terrier pair, 4½" x 7" ....$25.00 – 27.50
Terrier, 4" ....$15.00 – 17.50
Puppies in Basket, 2½" .....$12.50 – 15.00

5th Row:
Lady Bugs (3), 2¼" x 2½" ...$8.50 – 10.00 ea.
Monkeys, white (3), 1¾" ....$4.00 – 5.00 ea.
Monkeys (3), 2¼" ....$6.00 – 7.50 ea.
Monkeys, "Speak, see, and hear no
 evil" ....$10.00 – 12.50
Cat w/Fiddle, 2" ....$6.00 – 7.50
Rabbit, 1" x 2¼" ....$6.00 – 7.50

Page 10

Top Row:
Dogs ....$15.00 – 20.00 ea.
Bird ....$15.00 – 17.50
Frog (Bisque) ....$20.00 – 22.00

2nd Row:
Birds ....$7.50 – 9.00 ea.
Dog ....$10.00 – 12.00
Geese (Blue Base, Set 3).$18.00 – 22.00
Goose Grooming Feathers.....$6.00 – 7.50

3rd Row:
Bird..................................$2.00 – 3.00
Dog (Rubber).....................$8.00 – 10.00
Dog and Hydrant ....$10.00 – 12.50
Penguin ....$7.00 – 8.00
Dog with Ribbon ....$7.00 – 8.00

4th Row:
Dogs (First Three)..............$6.00 – 7.50 ea.
Dog (Gray Dachshund) .....$12.00 – 15.00
Dog (Celluloid) ....$6.00 – 8.00

5th Row:
Bird ....$3.00 – 4.00
Swan ....$3.00 – 4.00
Monkey ....$4.00 – 5.00
Deer ....$5.00 – 6.00
Duck (Humanoid) ....$15.00 – 20.00

Page 11

Top Row:
Chicken Pair ....$20.00 – 25.00
Dog ....$15.00 – 17.50
Woebegone Horse ....$10.00 – 12.50

2nd Row:
1st Dog, 7" ....$12.50 – 15.00
2nd and 3rd Dogs ....$12.50 – 15.00 ea.
Elephant...........................$10.00 – 12.00
Bird ....$15.00 – 17.50

3rd Row:
Frogs ....$15.00 – 17.50 ea.
Dog ....$8.00 – 10.00
Cat on Bed/Set...............$15.00 – 17.50
Lamb ....$6.00 – 7.00

Price Guide →

4th Row:

Frog ....$10.00 – 12.00
Dog/Set (3) ....$10.00 – 12.50
Rabbit/Set (4) Dated 1951 .$20.00 – 25.00

5th Row:

Lady Bugs ....$8.50 – 10.00 ea.
Elephants on Wood Set.....$20.00 – 25.00
Cat.............................$4.00 – 5.00
Cat (Black Celluloid) ....$10.00 – 12.00
Scotties (Celluloid) ....$8.00 – 10.00

Page 12

Top Row:

1st, Pony ....$6.00 – 8.00
2nd, Jumping Horses 5" ....$35.00 – 45.00
3rd and 4th, Horses..........$12.50 – 15.00 ea.
5th, Donkey ....$8.00 – 10.00
6th, Deer ....$2.50 – 4.00

2nd Row:

Metal Horse w/Saddle ......$10.00 – 12.50
Metal Donkey w/Prospecting
    Gear.....................$10.00 – 12.50
Saddle Horse w/Cork ....$10.00 – 12.50
Deer ....$6.00 – 8.00
Cow.............................$8.00 – 10.00
Goat............................$6.00 – 8.00

3rd Row:

1st, Lady Bug w/Bat, 2¼" ....$6.00 – 8.00
2nd and 3rd, Lady Bug w/Hat or
    Umbrella ....$5.00 – 6.00 ea.
4th, Lady Bug w/Newspaper$5.00 – 6.00
5th, Lady Bug w/Bass Fiddle and Top
    Hat, 3" ....$8.50 – 10.00
6th, Lady Bug w/Mandolin and Polka Dot
    Hat ....$8.50 – 10.00
7th, Lady Bug w/Horn and
    Turban ....$8.50 – 10.00
8th, Lady Bug w/Violin........$8.50 – 10.00
9th, Lady Bug w/Bag ....$8.50 – 10.00
10th, Lady Bug w/Accordion .$8.50 – 10.00

4th Row:

1st, Lady Bug w/Vest 3½" ..$8.50 – 10.00
2nd, Lady Bug Ice Man...$10.00 – 12.50
3rd, Lady Bug w/Lantern .$10.00 – 12.50
4th and 5th, Lady Bug w/Soda and
    Singer......................$8.50 – 10.00 ea.
6th, Lady Bug w/Buggy........$6.00 – 8.00
7th, Lady Bug w/Camera .$10.00 – 12.50

5th Row:

Lady Bug w/Bat, 4" ....$12.50 – 15.00
Lady Bug w/Broom ....$10.00 – 12.50
Lady Bug w/Umbrella.......$10.00 – 12.50
Lady Bug Indian w/Pipe..$12.50 – 15.00
Same marked ....$12.50 – 15.00
Lady Bug w/Newspaper ..$10.00 – 12.50
Lady Bug Hobo...............$10.00 – 12.50

Page 13

Top Row:

Seated Dog, 4⅜" ....$20.00 – 25.00
"Luster," Dog ....$10.00 – 12.50

Gray and White Dog.........$12.50 – 15.00
Bird Dogs.....................$30.00 – 35.00
5th, Standing Dog, 7⅛" .....$17.50 – 20.00

2nd Row:

1st, 4th, 5th, and 8th, Dogs .$15.00 – 17.50 ea.
2nd and 6th, Dogs ....$12.50 – 15.00 ea.
3rd, Collie....................$10.00 – 12.50
7th, Setter ....$15.00 – 17.50

3rd Row:

1st, 2nd, and 7th, Dogs ....$7.50 – 10.00 ea.
3rd, Scottie....................$10.00 – 12.50
4th and 6th ....$10.00 – 12.00 ea.
5th, Standing Dog ....$10.00 – 12.50

4th Row:

Standing ....$10.00 – 12.50
Scottie ....$12.50 – 15.00
Black and White...............$20.00 – 25.00
4th and 5th, Celluloid
    Scotties ....$8.00 – 10.00 ea.
Terrier ....$10.00 – 12.50
Scottie ....$12.50 – 15.00
Small ....$10.00 – 12.50

5th Row:

1st, 6th, and 7th, Groups.....$8.00 – 10.00 ea.
2nd, Big Ears ....$6.00 – 8.00
3rd and 4th, Basket Dogs,
    3" ....$10.00 – 12.50 ea.
5th, Scotties in Cart..........$15.00 – 17.50

Page 14

Top Row:

Cat Planter, 3⅝" ....$6.00 – 8.00
Cat Sitting ....$22.50 – 25.00
Cat Reclining...................$22.50 – 25.00
Cat Planter....................$6.00 – 8.00
Cat w/Bow ....$6.00 – 8.00

2nd Row:

Cat w/Pert Expression..........$2.50 – 4.00
Cat w/Kitten ....$2.50 – 4.00
Black Cat w/Basket.............$5.00 – 6.00
Cat w/Bee-like Tail ....$2.50 – 4.00
Cat w/Bow ....$4.00 – 5.00
Cat w/Paw Up ....$4.00 – 5.00
Cat w/Tail Up ....$5.00 – 6.00
Cat w/Tiger Tail ....$2.50 – 4.00
Black Cat (Celluloid) ....$6.00 – 8.00

3rd Row:

1st, Curly Tail Cat................$2.50 – 4.00
2nd – 4th, Set w/Ball, Yarn,
    Bug ....$2.00 – 3.00 ea.
5th and 7th, Cats in Potty......$2.00 – 3.00 ea.
6th, Cat w/Red Yarn ....$5.00 – 6.00
8th, Bull Dog with Rubber Tail .$7.50 – 10.00
9th, Dog Sitting ....$5.00 – 6.00
10th, Dog Walking...............$2.50 – 4.00

4th Row:

1st and 2nd, Yellow and Blue Dog
    Planters, 4" ....$5.00 – 6.00 ea.
3rd and 4th, Long Dogs ....$6.00 – 8.00

5th, Dog w/Hat and Pipe,
    3½"........................$10.00 – 12.50
6th, Dog, same except 2⅜"....$5.00 – 6.00

5th Row:

1st and 2nd, Brown or Black Dog
    Planters ....$5.00 – 6.00 ea.
3rd, Dog Sitting.................$8.00 – 10.00
4th, Spotted Dog Planter.......$5.00 – 6.00
5th and 6th, Dog Planters .....$5.00 – 6.00 ea.

Page 15

Top Row:

Large Bird, 7⅞" ....$30.00 – 35.00
Small Bird on Branch ....$2.00 – 3.00
Pair of Birds ....$10.00 – 12.50
Pair of Birds ....$8.00 – 10.00
Large Bird 7¾" ....$30.00 – 35.00

2nd Row:

Colorful Bird ....$12.50 – 15.00
Bird Bending...................$15.00 – 20.00
Bird on Branch ....$12.50 – 15.00
Small Birds on Branch.........$2.00 – 3.00
Blue Bird ....$4.00 – 5.00
Green Bird......................$6.00 – 8.00

3rd Row:

1st, 2nd, 3rd, and 5th, Stork or
    Pelican ....$6.00 – 8.00 ea.
4th, Swan......................$5.00 – 6.00
6th, Small Winged Bird.........$6.00 – 8.00
7th – 9th, Small Birds............$4.00 – 5.00 ea.

4th Row:

Geese.........................$6.00 – 7.50 ea.

5th Row:

1st – 8th, Musical "Donald
    Ducks"......................$10.00 – 12.00 ea.
9th – 11th, Musical Long-Billed
    Ducks ....$6.00 – 8.00 ea.

Page 16

Top Row:

Ducks, 5" to 6½" wall
    plaques.....................$22.50 – 25.00 ea.

2nd Row:

Chicken pr., 5".................$20.00 – 22.50
Bird, 3" ....$3.00 – 4.50
Ducks, 4".......................$10.00 – 12.50

3rd Row:

Jay, 2½" ....$4.00 – 5.00
Crane, 3¼".....................$6.00 – 8.00
Peacock, 3⅛"..................$6.00 – 8.00
Bird, 2¼".......................$3.00 – 4.00
Bird, 2½"......................$4.00 – 5.00

4th Row:

Peacock, 7" ....$25.00 – 27.50
Chicken on Nest, 5⅞",
    2 piece.....................$35.00 – 40.00
Flamingo, 5½" ....$12.50 – 15.00
Flamingo, 7¼" ....$25.00 – 27.50

5th Row:
Gazelles, 3¾" ....$7.00 – 8.50
Frog w/Mandolin, 3½" ......$17.50 – 20.00
Frog w/Violin, 4¼" ....$20.00 – 22.00
Frog w/Accordion, 4" ....$20.00 – 22.00
Penguin Bookends, pr., 4" .$20.00 – 25.00

Page 17

Top Row:
Plume-tailed Peacock, 5" ..$20.00 – 22.00
Flamingo............................$20.00 – 22.50
Bird..$2.50 – 4.00
Blue Birds..............................$7.50 – 10.00
Small Birds on Limb.............$2.00 – 3.00
Bird w/Long Tail...................$4.00 – 5.00
Penguin ....$6.00 – 7.00
Fancy Plume-tailed Peacock .$20.00 – 22.00

2nd Row:
1st and 2nd, Birds on Limb ...$2.00 – 3.00 ea.
3rd, Duck w/Hat ....$6.00 – 8.00
4th – 6th, Birds on Limb .....$7.50 – 10.00 ea.
7th, Birds on Stump ....$8.00 – 10.00

3rd Row:
1st and 3rd, Chick.................$2.00 – 3.00 ea.
2nd, Swan.............................$2.50 – 4.00
4th and 8th – 11th, Birds.......$2.50 – 4.00 ea.
5th – 7th, Birds ....$2.50 – 4.00 ea.

4th Row:
Frog w/Accordion.............$10.00 – 12.50
Frog w/Bass Fiddle ....$10.00 – 12.50
Frog on Lily Pad...............$17.50 – 20.00
Frog Drummer...................$17.50 – 20.00
Frog w/Accordion.............$17.50 – 20.00
6th and 7th, Frog w/Violin or
    Mandolin ....$15.00 – 17.50 ea.

5th Row:
Bear w/Hat.........................$8.00 – 10.00
Hugging Pandas ....$10.00 – 12.50
Brown Bear ....$10.00 – 12.50
Polar Bear (?) ....$5.00 – 6.00
Frog Ash Tray.....................$12.50 – 15.00
Frog Vase ....$12.50 – 15.00
Bisque Frog Fish Bowl
    Ornament ....$12.50 – 15.00
Reclining Frog...................$15.00 – 17.50

Page 18

Top Row:
Lion Pride, 4⅛" ....$45.00 – 50.00
Lion.......................................$5.00 – 6.00
Pig ....$8.00 – 10.00
4th, Seal...............................$6.00 – 8.00
5th, Squirrel ....$10.00 – 12.50
6th, Squirrel, pair.............$17.50 – 20.00

2nd Row:
Green Elephant, 3¾"........$15.00 – 17.50
Small Brown Elephant ....$7.50 – 10.00
Grayish-White Elephant, 4".$17.50 – 20.00
4th and 5th, Pink Elephants ..$4.00 – 5.00 ea.
Brown Elephants...............$10.00 – 12.50

Red Elephant ....$5.00 – 6.00
8th – 10th, Elephant Family Set,
    nice detail ....$60.00 – 80.00
    Large ....$25.00 – 30.00
    Medium...........................$20.00 – 25.00
    Small ....$15.00 – 20.00

3rd Row:
1st, 2nd, and 5th, Roosters....$6.00 – 7.00 ea.
3rd, Large Rooster, 3½" .....$8.00 – 10.00
4th, Chicken Family...........$20.00 – 25.00
6th, Butterfly ....$6.00 – 8.00

4th Row:
Monkey, missing piano, 3⅛"...$8.00 – 10.00
    w/piano ....$12.50 – 15.00
2nd and 3rd, Monkeys
    w/Instruments ....$12.50 – 15.00
Monkey w/Horn ....$6.00 – 8.00
Monkey w/Dark Brown Suit.$30.00 – 35.00
Three Monkey Set ....$10.00 – 12.00
Rabbit w/Drum..................$12.50 – 15.00
Rabbit w/Egg.......................$6.00 – 8.00
Lobster...............................$17.50 – 20.00

5th Row:
1st, 3rd, and 6th, Fish ....$6.00 – 8.00 ea.
Fish in Weeds.......................$5.00 – 6.00
Clams, open or closed ....$5.00 – 6.00 ea.
Bisque Bass ....$8.00 – 10.00
White Fish ....$5.00 – 6.00

Page 19

Top Row:
Swan, 4" x 5½", Lefton .....$40.00 – 50.00
Duck, 3½" x 6" ....$15.00 – 20.00
Duck, 3" x 5" ....$12.50 – 15.00

2nd Row:
Goose, 3½" ....$5.00 – 6.00
Bird on Tree Branch, 3"....$12.50 – 15.00 ea.
Rooster w/Cart, 3" x 4½"......$6.00 – 7.50
Birds in Tree, 3¼" x 4½"...$15.00 – 17.50

3rd Row:
Duck w/Scarf, 3¼" x 4" .....$8.00 – 10.50
Owl, 2½".............................$8.00 – 10.00
Swan, 2" ....$3.00 – 3.50
Duck w/Cart, 3" x 5"............$6.00 – 7.50
Donald Duck, 3"...............$12.50 – 15.00

4th Row:
Swan, 3" ....$5.00 – 6.00
Parrot, 6¼" ....$18.00 – 20.00
Duck w/Hat, 6½" x 6" ....$10.00 – 12.50
Duck Held by Child, 4"......$12.50 – 15.00

5th Row:
Bird w/House 3"...................$7.50 – 9.00
Birds on Flowers of Branch,
    3½" x 4½"....................$12.50 – 15.00 ea.
Flamingo, 3" ....$15.00 – 17.50

Page 20

Top Row:
Lady Duck in Bonnet Planter .$12.50 – 15.00

Male Duck in Top Hat
    Planter ....$12.50 – 15.00
Chicken Creamer ....$22.50 – 25.00
Goose Planter ....$12.50 – 15.00

2nd Row:
Cygnet Planter ....$8.00 – 10.00
Swan Planter ....$12.50 – 15.00
Swan Planter w/Wings
    Spread ....$15.00 – 17.50

3rd Row:
Chickens on Planter ....$5.00 – 6.00
Goose Planter ....$10.00 – 12.50
Chicken w/Egg Planter.....$15.00 – 17.50
Chick w/Basket Planter ....$5.00 – 6.00

4th Row:
Barnyard Goose Planter........$6.00 – 8.00
Rooster Pulling Egg Cart
    Planter ....$17.50 – 20.00
Blue Swan ....$8.00 – 10.00

5th Row:
1st, Green Geese Planter..$12.50 – 15.00
2nd, Goose and Goslings
    Planter ....$15.00 – 17.50
3rd, Duckling w/Basket Planter..$6.00 – 8.00
4th, Flamingo w/Basket
    Planter ....$10.00 – 12.50

Page 21

Top Row:
Mallard Planter................$15.00 – 17.00
Duckling Near Hatched Egg
    Planter ....$12.50 – 15.00
Duckling in Egg Planter ....$12.50 – 15.00

2nd Row:
Rooster, Two-piece Covered
    Jar ....$35.00 – 40.00
Smaller Rooster Jar..........$25.00 – 30.00
Long-Billed Bird Planter.......$5.00 – 6.00

3rd Row:
Goose Preening Planter ....$6.00 – 7.50
Chicken on Basket ....$30.00 – 35.00
Mallard Planter................$12.50 – 15.00

4th Row:
Small Duck Planter ....$4.00 – 5.00
Blue and Green Duck Planter..$4.00 – 5.00
Duck w/Wings Raised.......$10.00 – 12.50

5th Row:
Goose Planter ....$4.00 – 5.00
Duck w/Egg Cart ....$12.50 – 15.00
Blue and Green Duck ....$8.00 – 10.00
Chicken Pulling Cart ....$6.00 – 8.00

Page 22

Top Row:
1st, Parrot..........................$15.00 – 17.50
2nd and 3rd, Hanging Bird Planters
    w/24" chain ....$50.00 – 65.00 ea.
4th, Bird Planter ....$10.00 – 12.00

Price Guide —

2nd Row:
Elephant Planters..............$12.50 – 15.00 ea.

3rd Row:
1st, White Elephant Planter ..$5.00 – 6.00
2nd and 4th, Rearing
    Elephants ....$8.00 – 10.00 ea.
3rd, Brown Elephant........$15.00 – 18.00
5th and 6th, Smaller versions of second
    row ....$7.50 – 10.00 ea.

4th Row:
1st – 3rd, Birds on Fence, Cow, and
    Pig ....$8.00 – 10.00 ea.
4th Frog ....$18.00 – 20.00 ea.

5th Row:
1st – 3rd, Elephant or Bird
    Planters ....$8.00 – 10.00 ea.
4th, Bear on Blue Tree .....$10.00 – 12.50
5th, Blue Squirrel ....$8.00 – 10.00

Page 23

Top Row:
1st and 2nd, Lambs........$6.00 – 8.00 ea.
3rd, Hanging Parrot..........$35.00 – 45.00
4th, Parrot......................$18.00 – 20.00
5th, Hanging Parrot w/24"
    chain............................$50.00 – 65.00

2nd Row:
1st – 3rd, Lambs ....$12.50 – 15.00 set
4th, Lamb.........................$2.50 – 4.00
5th, Pink Bunny................$10.00 – 12.50
6th and 7th, Bunnies.......$10.00 – 12.50 ea.

3rd Row:
1st, Woodpecker Eyeing Frog.$5.00 – 6.00
2nd – 4th, Birds ....$6.00 – 8.00 ea.
5th, Green Donkey ....$6.00 – 8.00

4th Row:
1st, Medium Donkey.............$6.00 – 8.00
2nd – 8th, except 6th............$3.00 – 5.00 ea.
6th, Donkey ....$4.00 – 5.00

5th Row:
1st, Zebra ....$6.00 – 8.00
2nd, Dog Cart.......................$5.00 – 6.00
3rd, Very Small Donkey Cart..$2.00 – 3.00
4th and 5th, Cow Carts .....$7.50 – 10.00 ea.
6th, Cow Planter ....$6.00 – 8.00

Page 24

Top Row:
Donkey w/Green Cart Planter.$12.50 – 15.00
Donkey w/Floral Cart Planter ..$9.00 – 11.00
Donkey w/Brown Cart Planter.$8.00 – 10.00

2nd Row:
Donkey w/Cart Planter .....$10.00 – 12.50
Pack Mule Planter ....$10.00 – 12.50
Same as above with different
    coloring.......................$10.00 – 12.50

3rd Row:
Donkey w/Cart Planter ....$8.00 – 10.00

Donkey w/Cart Planter ....$8.00 – 10.00
Siesta Time w/Donkey
    Planter ....$12.50 – 15.00

4th Row:
Donkey Pulling Cart
    Planters ....$7.50 – 10.00 ea.

5th Row:
1st, Donkey w/Two Basket
    Planters....................$5.00 – 6.00
2nd, Zebra w/Basket Planter .$6.00 – 8.00
3rd, Blue Striped Donkey w/Two
    Baskets ....$6.00 – 8.00
4th and 5th, Zebras w/Basket.$5.00 – 6.00 ea.
6th, Spotted Horse (?)
    w/Basket........................$5.00 – 6.00

Page 25

Top Row:
Brown Dog Planter, 3⅝"........$4.00 – 5.00
Black Dog Planter, 4⅝".........$6.00 – 8.00
Same, orange.......................$6.00 – 8.00
Same, blue...........................$6.00 – 8.00
Same as 1st, black................$4.00 – 5.00

2nd Row:
Brown Dog, 3⅝", w/Top Hat
    Planter.........................$8.00 – 10.00
Same, black and white ....$8.00 – 10.00
Dog Planter.......................$17.50 – 20.00
Spotted Dog w/Basket
    Planter ....$5.00 – 6.00
Dog w/Spotted Basket
    Planter ....$6.00 – 8.00

3rd Row:
Dog w/Blue Ribbon and Planter.$5.00 – 6.00
Dog w/Jaws Tied, 1½" ....$5.00 – 6.00
Same, only 2⅝" ....$7.50 – 10.00
Dog w/Green Basket Planter .$6.00 – 8.00
Dog Resting on Sack ....$6.00 – 8.00
Pair of Dogs.......................$6.00 – 8.00
Dog at Fire Plug ....$8.00 – 10.00

4th Row:
Standing Dog ....$17.50 – 20.00
Bird Dog ....$7.50 – 10.00
Dog Holding Ball.............$7.50 – 10.00
Dog Holding Ball..............$10.00 – 12.50
Setter ....$12.50 – 15.00
Bull Dog..........................$17.50 – 20.00

5th Row:
Begging Dog ....$2.50 – 4.00
Dog w/Blue Ribbon ....$5.00 – 6.00
Spotted Dog ....$6.00 – 8.00
Bull Dog in Red Hat.........$12.50 – 15.00
Brown Dog..........................$6.00 – 8.00
Group of Three Dogs........$12.50 – 15.00
Sitting Dog ....$12.50 – 15.00
Dog w/Bug on Nose ....$7.50 – 10.00
Poodle w/Rose Hat..........$15.00 – 17.50

Page 26

Top Row:
1st – 4th, Swan Set.........$90.00 – 120.00

Small Swan.....................$15.00 – 20.00 ea.
Large Swan.....................$40.00 – 50.00
Swan Box ....$20.00 – 30.00

2nd Row:
Black Cigarette Box w/Floral
    Top ....$22.50 – 25.00
Cigarette Box w/Applied
    Roses ....$20.00 – 22.50
Black Cigarette Box w/Floral
    Top ....$22.50 – 25.00

3rd Row:
Ash Tray w/Bird ....$12.50 – 15.00
2nd – 4th, Ash Trays for above
    boxes ....$8.00 – 10.00 ea.
Fish Ash Tray ....$7.50 – 10.00

4th Row:
Black Cigarette Box
    w/Orchid ....$30.00 – 35.00
2nd Children Ash Trays........$5.00 – 6.00 ea.
Pagoda Scene Box ....$30.00 – 35.00
4th, Children Ash Trays........$5.00 – 6.00

5th Row:
House on Lake Scene Ash
    Tray ....$7.50 – 10.00
Flower Cigarette Holder....$17.50 – 20.00
Chamber Pot ....$5.00 – 6.00
Swan w/Tail Cigarette Rest..$6.00 – 8.00

Page 27

Top Row:
1st and 4th, Man Carrying Dragon-lidded Box,
6⅜"......................................$25.00 – 27.50 ea.
2nd, Georgia Map Ash
    Tray ....$12.50 – 15.00
3rd, Knight w/Shield Ash
    Tray ....$6.00 – 8.00

2nd Row:
Green Floral Cigarette Box w/Two Ash
    Trays.........................$20.00 – 25.00 set
Violet Cigarette Box w/Two Ash
    Trays.........................$30.00 – 40.00 set
Dragon Decoration Cigarette Box w/Two
    Ash Trays...................$35.00 – 40.00 set

3rd Row:
Ash Tray in Hummel-like
    Design ....$10.00 – 12.50
Ash Tray to match first box, second
    row ....$2.00 – 3.00
Children in House Ash Tray..$4.00 – 5.00
Ash Tray to match second box,
    second row ....$2.50 – 4.00
Chicken Ash Tray ....$6.00 – 7.00
Ash Tray to match third box,
    second row ....$3.00 – 5.00

4th Row:
Cigarette Box w/Pink Rose .$10.00 – 12.50
"Loop over Great Smokies" ..$10.00 – 12.50
Diamond Ash Tray..............$2.00 – 3.00
Coal Hod Match Holder....$10.00 – 12.50

Coal Hod Match Holder w/Floral
   Scene ....$10.00 – 12.50
Moss and Rose Cigarette
   Box ....$8.00 – 10.00

5th Row:
Pink Embossed Rose Cigarette
   Box ....$10.00 – 12.50
Blue Floral Cigarette Box .$10.00 – 12.50
Swirled Floral Cigarette Box ..$10.00 – 12.50
Florida Ash Tray ....$12.50 – 15.00

Page 28
Top Row:
New York Crumb Pan.......$10.00 – 12.50
Ornate Swan Crumb Pan .$17.50 – 20.00
Floral Crumb Pan............$10.00 – 12.50
Small Floral Crumb Pan........$5.00 – 6.00

2nd Row:
Ash Tray, St. Joseph ....$2.50 – 4.00
Ash Tray, Birmingham.........$2.50 – 4.00
Ash Tray, Boys Town..........$6.00 – 8.00
Ash Tray, Sailboat..............$2.50 – 4.00
Ash Tray, Football ....$5.00 – 6.00

3rd Row:
Ash Tray, Pikes Peak..........$2.50 – 4.00
Ash Tray, Wisconsin Dells ....$2.50 – 4.00
Ash Tray, New York City .$10.00 – 12.50
Ash Tray, Washington, D.C. $2.50 – 4.00

4th Row:
Ash Tray, Hollywood ....$2.50 – 4.00
Ash Tray, Hannibal, Mo. ......$2.50 – 4.00
Ash Tray, Washington, D.C. ...$2.50 – 4.00
Ash Tray, Long Beach ....$2.50 – 4.00

5th Row:
Buddha Box ....$20.00 – 25.00
Pagoda Box ....$20.00 – 25.00
Cupid Box.......................$15.00 – 20.00
Red Box w/Sterling Silver
   Decoration....................$20.00 – 25.00

Page 29
Top Row:
Buddha Tray...................$10.00 – 12.00
New York City Souvenir Tray .$6.00 – 9.00
Ornate Serving Tray.........$12.50 – 15.00

2nd Row:
1st, Louisiana Souvenir Tray.$4.00 – 5.00
2nd, New York Heart w/Statue
   of Liberty ....$10.00 – 12.50
3rd, 5th and 6th, Ash Trays..$2.00 – 3.00 ea.
4th, Ash Tray.....................$2.50 – 4.00

3rd Row:
Candy, three part..............$10.00 – 12.50
Florida Souvenir Tray ....$4.00 – 5.00
Chicago Souvenir Tray ....$4.00 – 5.00
Ornate Gold-colored Ash Tray .$4.00 – 5.00
Ornate Silver-plated Ash Tray ..$6.00 – 7.00

4th Row:
Oval Tray.........................$5.00 – 6.00

Ash Tray w/Peacock...........$2.50 – 4.00
Six-piece Cigarette Set.....$20.00 – 25.00
Yellowstone Park Souvenir
   Tray ....$4.00 – 5.00

5th Row:
Colorado Souvenir Tray ....$4.00 – 5.00
Howe Cabins NY ....$4.00 – 5.00
Ornate Blue Ash Tray ....$4.00 – 5.00
Six-piece Miniature Tea Set .$15.00 – 20.00
El Paso, c. 1950 ....$5.00 – 6.00

Page 30
Top Row:
Gun Lighter w/Pearl
   Handles ....$17.50 – 20.00
Gun Lighter on Tripod.......$12.50 – 15.00
Small Gun Lighter..............$7.50 – 10.00
Large Gun Lighter on Base..$17.50 – 20.00
Small Pearl Handle Lighter.$8.00 – 10.00
Pearl Handle Lighter on
   Base..........................$15.00 – 17.50
Gun Lighter on Base..........$8.00 – 10.00

2nd Row:
Baby Table Lighter in Box ....$6.00 – 8.00
Hand Lighter.....................$12.50 – 15.00
Champagne Bucket Lighter ..$15.00 – 17.50
Urn Lighter ....$8.00 – 10.00
Pin Lighter w/Jewels and
   Pearls ....$15.00 – 20.00
Gun Lighter...........................$6.00 – 8.00
Gun Lighter with Base ....$8.00 – 10.00
Gun Lighter........................$10.00 – 12.50
Pearl Handle Gun Lighter.$12.50 – 15.00

3rd Row:
1st Bottle Lighter................$8.00 – 10.00
2nd and 3rd, Genie Lamps .$12.50 – 15.00 ea.
4th, Basket of Fruit ....$10.00 – 12.50
5th and 6th, Set................$25.00 – 30.00 set

4th Row:
1st, Heart Ring Box ....$10.00 – 12.50
2nd, Silent Butler, paper label.$7.50 – 10.00
3rd, Box..............................$8.00 – 10.00
4th, Cornucopia on Tray,
   both ....$15.00 – 17.50 set
5th Horse Head Ash Tray .$10.00 – 12.50

5th Row:
1st, Large Book Box.........$12.50 – 15.00
2nd, Small Book Box ....$10.00 – 12.50
3rd – 5th, Piano Boxes......$15.00 – 20.00 ea.
6th, Piano Box ....$15.00 – 17.50
7th, Piano Box ....$12.50 – 15.00

Page 31
Top Row:
Ash Tray w/Lighter ....$20.00 – 22.50
Celluloid Piano ....$25.00 – 30.00
Metal Piano......................$20.00 – 25.00
"Photolite" Table Lighter....$35.00 – 40.00
Golf Ball Lighter ....$15.00 – 18.00

2nd Row:
Knight Lighter ....$10.00 – 15.00

Knight Lighter ....$10.00 – 15.00
Camel Lighter ....$15.00 – 20.00
Elephant Lighter ....$15.00 – 20.00
Rocket Ship Lighter ....$30.00 – 35.00
Scottie Dog Lighter..........$17.50 – 20.00

3rd Row:
Fish Lighter......................$12.50 – 15.00
Desk Lighter ....$5.00 – 6.00
Normal-style Lighter ....$6.00 – 8.00
Aladdin-type Lighter ....$6.00 – 8.00
Lighter..............................$5.00 – 6.00
Desk Lighter ....$6.00 – 8.00

4th Row:
Peacock Lighter...............$10.00 – 12.50
Fancy Dragon Six-piece Cigarette
   Set ....$35.00 – 40.00
Floor Model Radio Lighter .$20.00 – 25.00
Barrel "Chicago" ....$10.00 – 12.50

5th Row:
1st – 3rd, Horse Head
   Lighters ....$12.50 – 15.00 ea.
Boot Lighter with Ash Tray ..$8.00 – 10.00
Two Boots w/Hat Ash
   Tray ....$15.00 – 17.50 set

Page 32
Top Row:
Man, 15½" ....$150.00 – 175.00
Lady, 14½" ....$125.00 – 150.00

2nd Row:
Cupid and Swan ....$35.00 – 40.00
Cupid Artist ....$75.00 – 90.00
Cupid Standing ....$35.00 – 40.00

3rd Row:
"Hummel-like" Boy and Girl ..$25.00 – 35.00 ea.
Cupid and Heart ....$75.00 – 90.00
Seated Musician ....$30.00 – 35.00

Page 33
Top:
Planter Couple w/Rabbits,
   5¼" x 7¼".................$125.00 – 150.00

Right:
Cupid w/Gold Rings and Lady w/Lyre,
   8¼" x 9¼".......................$250.00 – 300.00

Bottom:
Courting Couple w/Lambs,
   8¼" x 9¼".................$300.00 – 350.00

Page 34
Top Row:
Colonial Man, 7"...............$27.50 – 30.00
Colonial Man, 7"...............$27.50 – 30.00
Lady w/Basket, 7" ....$35.00 – 37.50
Lady w/Dog, 6"................$22.50 – 25.00
Man, 6½".........................$17.50 – 20.00
Windy Lady, 6½".............$25.00 – 27.50

2nd Row:
Couple, 3½".....................$15.00 – 17.50

Lady w/Basket, 6" ....$22.50 – 25.00
Lady Shell Planter,
5½" x 6½" ....$55.00 – 65.00
Dancer, 5" ....$15.00 – 17.50

3rd Row:
Lady, 4¾" ....$15.00 – 17.50
Lady, 4" ....$12.50 – 15.00
Horn Player, 4½" ....$15.00 – 17.50
Colonial Man, 5"................$12.50 – 15.00
Lady w/Goose, 5⅝" ....$55.00 – 65.00

4th Row:
Lady w/Fan, 10½" ....$75.00 – 85.00
Lady, 10¼" ....$60.00 – 65.00
Man w/Flowers, 10¼".......$60.00 – 65.00
Man w/Violin, 9"................$55.00 – 60.00

Page 35

Top Row:
Orientals, 6"....$20.00 ea./$45.00 – 50.00 pr.
Seated Colonials,
7" ....$72.50 ea./$145.00 – 160.00 pr.
Country Couple, 6¼" male and 6" f
emale ....$20.00 ea./$40.00 – 45.00 pr.

2nd Row:
1st and 6th pr. Vase,
5" ....$22.50 ea./$50.00 – 55.00 pr.
Couple, 9¼" ..$50.00 ea./$100.00 – 110.00 pr.
Fence-Leaning Couple,
9" ....$60.00 ea./$120.00 – 130.00 pr.

3rd Row:
Flower Gatherers,
10¼"........$75.00 ea./$150.00 – 160.00 pr.
Plumed Hat Couple,
9¾" ....$60.00 ea./$120.00 – 130.00 pr.
Pastoral Couple,
10¼" ....$65.00 ea./$130.00 – 140.00 pr.

Page 36

Top Row:
1st, Lady Planter, 6" ....$60.00 – 75.00
2nd and 3rd, Cart Planters,
7"..............................$150.00 – 175.00 pr.
4th and 5th, Couple, 6½"...$30.00 – 40.00 pr.

2nd Row:
1st and 2nd, Tree Vases,
4½"...............................$20.00 – 25.00 pr.
3rd, Dancer.........................$8.00 – 10.00
4th and 5th, Musicians,
4½"...............................$12.50 – 15.00 ea.
6th Drummer, 4½" ....$12.50 – 15.00
7th, Boy w/Rabbit ....$10.00 – 12.50
8th and 9th, Couple, 4¼"...$20.00 – 25.00 pr

3rd Row:
1st and 2nd, Couple, 5⅜"..$30.00 – 40.00 pr.
3rd, Kid Couple Planter ....$50.00 – 60.00
4th, Sunflower Kids ....$60.00 – 75.00
5th and 6th, Colonial
Couple ....$30.00 – 35.00 pr.

4th Row:
1st and 2nd, Couple with Dogs,
7⅛".............................$90.00 – 100.00 pr.

3rd, Horse w/Rider, 10¼"..$175.00 – 200.00
4th and 5th, Couple, 7¼"...$80.00 – 90.00 pr.

Page 37

Top Row:
Bride and Groom, 6⅛" ......$45.00 – 50.00
Lady w/Basket, 6½" ....$25.00 – 30.00
Plaque, 6¼" ....$30.00 – 35.00
Plaque, 6¾" ....$40.00 – 45.00
Man Holding Hat, 6" ....$25.00 – 30.00
Lady w/Dog and Gun ....$25.00 – 30.00

2nd Row:
1st, Dancers, 3"................$10.00 – 12.50
2nd, Bride and Groom, 4¼" .$20.00 – 25.00
3rd and 4th, Planter Pair, 5¼".$75.00 – 100.00 pr.
5th, Child Playing Accordion,
2¾"..............................$10.00 – 12.50
6th, Boy w/Puppy ....$12.50 – 15.00

3rd Row:
1st, Man w/Umbrella, 3⅝" ..$12.50 – 15.00
2nd and 7th, Man and
Woman ....$10.00 – 12.50 ea.
3rd, Lady, 5"....................$12.50 – 15.00
4th, Couple, 5⅝"...............$35.00 – 40.00
5th, Seated Couple w/Dog,
3⅝"..............................$12.50 – 15.00
6th, Wall Pocket, 2⅜".........$8.00 – 10.00
8th, Child w/Instrument ....$10.00 – 12.50

4th Row:
1st and 2nd, Planter Couple,
6¼"..............................$30.00 – 40.00 pr.
3rd and 4th, Planters, 6" ...$60.00 – 75.00 ea.
5th, Fisherman, 7" ....$35.00 – 40.00
6th, Man w/Cape, 6".........$25.00 – 30.00

Page 38

Top Row:
1st, Lady w/Blue Hat, 5" ..$15.00 – 17.50
2nd, Lady w/Pink Hat, 5" .$15.00 – 17.50
3rd and 4th, Lady w/Fruit and Man
w/Flowers, 6⅜" ....$40.00 – 50.00 pr.
5th, Man Playing Flute......$15.00 – 17.50
6th, Lady in Blue Dress ....$15.00 – 17.50

2nd Row:
Girl w/Feather in Hair, 4⅜"..$12.50 – 15.00
Man w/Rake ....$12.50 – 15.00
Bootie...............................$7.50 – 10.00
Colonial Man in Beige Pants .$12.50 – 15.00
5th and 6th, Wall Pockets,
3⅝"..............................$25.00 – 30.00 pr.

3rd Row:
1st and 2nd, Colonial Man and
Lady, 4⅜" ....$30.00 – 35.00 pr.
3rd and 4th, Couple w/Urns,
5"................................$75.00 – 85.00 pr.
5th and 6th, White Couple,
4¼"..............................$25.00 – 30.00 pr.

4th Row:
1st and 2nd, Pastoral Couple by Fence,
8⅛"..........................$100.00 – 125.00 pr.

3rd, Lamp Couple, 7¼".....$50.00 – 60.00
4th and 5th, Musician Couple
7⅝"..............................$60.00 – 65.00 pr.

Page 39

Canisters .$25.00 – 30.00 ea./$150.00 – 180.00 set

Page 40

Stork ....$75.00 – 100.00

Page 41

Top Row:
Pink Crocheted Dress, 6"..$40.00 – 45.00
Nude, 4¾".........................$12.50 – 15.00
Pink Baby, 5½" ....$22.50 – 25.00

2nd Row:
Feather or Go Go Dancer, 13"..$40.00 – 45.00

3rd Row:
Yellow and White Crocheted Dress,
8".................................$45.00 – 50.00
Kewpie, 2¾"......................$17.50 – 20.00
Feather Dancer, 4¼".........$12.50 – 15.00
Blue Crocheted Suit, 7".....$45.00 – 50.00

Page 42

Top Row:
Dog ....$10.00 – 12.50
Lamb....................................$6.00 – 8.00
Cow.....................................$6.00 – 8.00
Goat....................................$6.00 – 8.00
Dog ....$8.00 – 10.00

2nd Row:
1st and 2nd, Goats...............$6.00 – 8.00 ea.
3rd and 5th, Donkey or
Horse ....$8.00 – 10.00 ea.
4th, Horse ....$10.00 – 12.00

3rd Row:
1st, 2nd, 6th, Jungle Cats ...$8.00 – 10.00 ea.
3rd and 7th, Leopards ......$10.00 – 12.50 ea.
4th and 5th, Tiger or Lion..$10.00 – 12.00 ea.

4th Row:
Snowsuited Baby, Jointed.$40.00 – 50.00
Nodding Head Donkey......$30.00 – 35.00
Nodding Head Donkey......$30.00 – 35.00
Snowsuited Baby ....$35.00 – 45.00

5th Row:
1st, Green Snowsuited
Baby ....$25.00 – 30.00
2nd, Yellow Snowsuited Jointed Body
Baby ....$30.00 – 40.00
3rd, Red-headed Baby .....$30.00 – 40.00
4th, U. S. Navy Doll ....$25.00 – 30.00

Page 43

Top Row:
Football Players, 6" ....$12.00 – 15.00 ea.

2nd Row:
1st, Baby in Crocheted Dress..$35.00 – 45.00
2nd – 4th, Rose Surprise.......$4.00 – 5.00 ea.
5th – 8th, Football Players,
4"...................................$8.00 – 10.00 ea.

9th, Rickshaw....................$10.00 – 12.50

3rd Row:
Zoo Animals......................$8.00 – 10.00 ea.

4th Row:
Kewpie w/Feathers ....$22.50 – 25.00
"Betty Boop," 8" ....$30.00 – 40.00
"Betty Boop," 6" ....$20.00 – 25.00
Baby, 11¾", moveable arms and
    legs................................$75.00 – 90.00
Dutch Girl, 8⅝" ....$40.00 – 50.00
Kewpie, 6½" ....$35.00 – 40.00

5th Row:
Black Hula Dancer w/Bows .$35.00 – 40.00
Stork in Cage Window
    Bobber ....$17.50 – 20.00
Clown................................$17.50 – 20.00
Baby ....$12.50 – 15.00
Pink Snow Baby ....$15.00 – 17.50
Baby Rattle.....................$20.00 – 22.50

Page 44
Top Row:
Water Lily in Box ....$7.50 – 10.00 ea.

2nd Row:
Dolls in Basket, 4⅝" x 3"...$60.00 – 65.00
Quints in Box, 2¾" ....$100.00 – 110.00

3rd Row:
Dog, Squeaker....................$8.00 – 10.00
Doll, China, 3¼" ....$25.00 – 30.00
Doll, China, 3" ....$17.50 – 20.00
Doll, Black, 3¼" ....$40.00 – 45.00
Doll, 7" ....$55.00 – 65.00

4th Row:
Ducks, 4" w/Hangers and Spring
    Legs ....$6.00 – 7.50
Magnifying Glass ....$10.00 – 12.50

5th Row:
Shell w/Paper Flowers, 1¼" .$2.50 – 3.00

6th Row:
Water Lily ....$7.50 – 10.00
Celluloid Dog House..........$10.00 – 12.50
Celluloid "Happy House" Pencil
    Holder ....$20.00 – 25.00
Paper Monkey Squeeze Accordion,
    1½" x 2½".....................$3.00 – 3.50
Celluloid Swan, 4½" ....$17.50 – 20.00

Page 45
Two Place Setting of 9 pcs ....$30.00 – 35.00
Four Place Setting of 13 pcs .$50.00 – 55.00
Six Place Setting of 23 pcs .$100.00 – 120.00
Six Place Setting of 26 pcs .$125.00 – 150.00
*Add $10.00 to 15.00 for box in good condition.

Top Row:
1st, Blue Pottery-Like Creamer .$6.00 – 8.00
2nd and 4th, Same Cup and
    Saucer ....$8.00 – 10.00

4th, Floral Lustre Creamer..$8.00 – 10.00
5th, Same Sugar w/Lid.....$10.00 – 12.50
6th, Doll's Nursing Set ......$60.00 – 75.00

2nd Row:
Camel Cup/Saucer ....$10.00 – 12.50
Miniature Eight Piece Set .$10.00 – 12.00
Miniature Six Piece Set ....$15.00 – 17.50
Miniature Ten Piece Set....$22.50 – 25.00
Blue Willow Gravy and Liner .$55.00 – 60.00

3rd Row:
1st, Lustre Sugar ....$6.00 – 8.00
2nd and 3rd, Creamers ....$6.00 – 8.00 ea.
4th, Yellow Floral Four-Piece
    Set ....$55.00 – 60.00

4th Row:
1st, Set, Orange Lustre, Two Piece
    Set in Box ....$30.00 – 35.00
2nd, Set, Elephant Set Plate .$10.00 – 12.00
Same Cup and Saucer......$10.00 – 12.00
Same Sugar w/Lid...........$12.50 – 15.00
Same Teapot w/Lid ....$17.50 – 20.00
Same Creamer................$10.00 – 12.00
3rd, Miniature Seven-Piece
    Set ....$25.00 – 30.00

5th Row:
Seventeen Piece Set in Box .$80.00 – 90.00
Thirteen Piece Set in Box .$60.00 – 70.00

Page 46
Top Row (Blue Willow):
Creamer, 1½" to 2"...........$12.50 – 15.00
Cup and Saucer, 2¾" to 3½" .$15.00 – 17.50
Plate, 3¾" to 4½" ....$12.00 – 15.00
Sugar w/Lid, 2" to 2¼" .....$17.50 – 20.00
Teapot w/Lid, 3¼" to 3¾" .$40.00 – 45.00

2nd Row:
Lustre ware: 4 piece setting .$65.00 – 75.00
Lustre Creamer, 1½"...........$6.00 – 7.50
Platter, Blue Willow, 6" ....$40.00 – 45.00
Tomato Teapot, 2" x 4"......$15.00 – 20.00
Tomato Cup and Saucer .....$7.50 – 10.00
Tomato Sugar w/Lid,
    1½" x 2".....................$10.00 – 12.00
Tomato Creamer (not shown) .$7.50 – 10.00

3rd Row:
Chest, 1½" high ....$6.00 – 7.50
Set: "Pico" w/2¾"tray, teapot, creamer and sugar,
    2 cups and saucers ....$22.50 – 25.00
Bench, 1¾" ....$4.00 – 5.00
Refrigerator, 3½" ....$18.00 – 20.00
Set: 2¼" tray, w/cr/sug.....$10.00 – 12.50
Sink, 2" x 3" ....$18.00 – 20.00
Set: tray, teapot, pitcher, cups and saucers,
    cr/sug ....$20.00 – 22.50
Set: teapot, cr/sug, 4 cups and
    saucers ....$22.50 – 25.00
Refrigerator, Philco, 2½"...$12.50 – 15.00
Cabinet, 2¼" ....$10.00 – 12.50
Dry Sink, 2" ....$10.00 – 12.50

Sets: as shown marked
    HKATO......................$15.00 – 17.50

4th Row:
Chair, 3"...........................$8.00 – 10.00
Chest, 1¾" ....$7.50 – 9.00
Couch, 3"..........................$15.00 – 17.50
Chair, 3"...........................$10.00 – 12.50
Dresser, 2⅛".....................$6.00 – 7.00
Chair, 1⅞".........................$5.00 – 6.00
Piano, 1¾".........................$7.50 – 9.00
Set: 1½" chest, 2¼" bed, 1¾"
    lamp ....$15.00 – 17.50

5th Row:
Elephant w/Flag Cup, 1¾" .$10.00 – 12.00
Same, Sugar w/Lid, 2½" ..$10.00 – 12.50
Same, Creamer, 1½"........$10.00 – 12.00
Set: 1½" teapot, creamer, sug w/lid
    (not shown).................$20.00 – 22.00
Set: teapot, creamer, 2 cups and saucers,
    sugar with lid (not shown).$25.00 – 28.00

6th Row:
Set: sugar w/lid, creamer (not shown), 4 cups
    and saucers..................$45.00 – 50.00
Set: sugar w/lid, creamer, 4 cups and
    saucers ....$55.00 – 65.00

Page 47
Top Row:
Chair w/Roses, 3" ....$10.00 – 12.50
Matching Couch, 3"..........$15.00 – 17.50
Chair w/Roses ....$10.00 – 12.50
Matching Stool ....$6.00 – 8.00
Dresser ....$12.50 – 15.00
Colonial Scene Couch ....$17.50 – 20.00
Matching Chair ....$12.50 – 15.00

2nd Row:
1st and 2nd, Chair and Stool w/Blue
    Rose ....$17.50 – 20.00 set
3rd and 4th, Chair w/Stool to
    match..........................$10.00 – 12.50 set
5th and 6th, Chair w/Stool to
    match..........................$12.50 – 15.00 set
7th, Clock Chair ....$12.50 – 15.00
8th – 10th, Lamps ....$8.00 – 10.00 ea.

3rd Row:
1st and 2nd, Bottles ....$4.00 – 5.00 ea.
3rd, GE Philco Refrigerator,
    2½"..............................$12.50 – 15.00
4th, Matching Cabinet w/Dishes,
    2¼"..............................$10.00 – 12.00
5th, Matching Stove ....$12.50 – 15.00
6th, Matching Dry Sink, 2" .$10.00 – 12.50
7th, Tub ....$8.00 – 10.00
8th, Pitcher w/Dragon..........$6.00 – 8.00
9th, Phone ....$7.50 – 10.00
10th, Cup and Saucer...........$6.00 – 8.00

4th Row:
1st, Blue Set on Tray ....$17.50 – 20.00
2nd, Tray Set...................$20.00 – 22.50
3rd and 5th, Luster Cup........$3.00 – 5.00 ea.

Price Guide ~

4th, Luster Sugar w/Lid........$5.00 – 7.00
5th, Orange Luster Plate ......$4.00 – 5.00
6th, Set: Teapot, Creamer, and
    Sugar ....$20.00 – 25.00

5th Row:
1st and 2nd, Casserole......$75.00 – 85.00
3rd, Tiny Set Creamer and Sugar on
    Tray ....$6.00 – 8.00
4th, Marching Toy Soldiers...$6.00 – 8.00
5th and 6th, Toy Soldiers on
    Horse.........................$6.00 – 8.00 ea.

Page 48
Tea Sets - Place Settings (Triple for Donald):
Two ....$30.00 – 35.00
Three ....$40.00 – 45.00
Four ....$50.00 – 55.00
Four with Tureen and
    Platter ....$90.00 – 95.00
Five ....$85.00 – 90.00
Six..............................$100.00 – 120.00
Tray, Sugar, Creamer,
    Teapot ....$25.00 – 30.00
Tray, Sugar, and Creamer .$17.50 – 20.00
Bath Set, 3 Pieces ....$30.00 – 35.00

Page 49
Place Settings:
Two ....$30.00 – 35.00
Three ....$40.00 – 45.00
Four ....$50.00 – 55.00
Four w/Tureen and Platter .$90.00 – 95.00
Five ....$85.00 – 90.00
Six..............................$100.00 – 120.00

Page 50
Left:
Cuckoo Clock..............$550.00 – 650.00

Right:
Pendulum Clock ....$350.00 – 400.00

Page 51
Top:
Bisque Clock w/Angels, 11¼".$600.00 – 700.00

Bottom:
Anniversary Clock, Girl in
    Swing ....$100.00 – 125.00

Page 52 top
Bisque Clock...................$80.00 – 100.00

Page 52 bottom
Top Row:
Reclining Clown ....$35.00 – 40.00
Clown Doing Hand Stand .$35.00 – 40.00
Clown in Striped Suit, 5¼".$35.00 – 40.00
Clown Playing Bass Fiddle.$15.00 – 17.50
Clown, 5"...................$15.00 – 17.50
Reclining Clown ....$35.00 – 40.00

Bottom Row:
Clown Playing Saxophone.$10.00 – 12.00
2nd – 4th, Clown w/Vase.....$8.00 – 10.00 ea.

5th and 6th, Clown Salt and Pepper
    Set ....$40.00 – 50.00 set

Page 53
Top Row:
Sets of Green, Blue, and
    Pink...........................$20.00 – 22.50 ea.

2nd Row:
"Capo di Monte"-type Plate.$12.50 – 15.00
Set, w/dancing girls ....$25.00 – 30.00
Set, w/dancing girls ....$30.00 – 35.00
Demitasse, 1¼" ....$20.00 – 22.50

3rd Row:
Set, red hearts w/black trim .$10.00 – 12.00
Set, blue w/floral ....$10.00 – 12.50
Set, black w/gold trim ....$12.50 – 15.00
Set, blue and white ....$12.50 – 15.00

4th Row:
Set ....$10.00 – 12.00
Set, black and white checkerboard
    border..........................$5.00 – 6.00
Set, blue rim ....$6.00 – 7.00
Set, Florida souvenir ....$8.00 – 10.00

5th Row:
Set, ladies w/red rim ....$20.00 – 22.50
Set, yellow rim flower ....$10.00 – 12.00
Demitasse White Floral .....$10.00 – 12.00
Set ....$10.00 – 12.00

Page 54
Top Row:
1st set "Merit"..................$10.00 – 12.50
2nd set "MIOJ"..............$10.00 – 12.50
3rd and 4th sets "Ucago"...$12.50 – 15.00
Blue flowered cup "Trimont
    China"...........................$6.00 – 7.50
5th set "Gold Castle" ....$10.00 – 12.50

2nd Row:
1st set "MIOJ"..................$18.00 – 20.00
2nd set "MIOJ"..............$20.00 – 22.00
Orange Dragon Cup........$12.50 – 15.00
3rd set "Lucky China" ....$17.50 – 20.00
4th set "MIOJ"..............$18.00 – 20.00
5th set "Sak China" ....$17.50 – 20.00
6th set "Gold China" ....$10.00 – 12.50

3rd Row:
1st set "MIOJ"..................$10.00 – 12.00
2nd set "Merit"..................$8.00 – 10.00
3rd set "Saji Fancy China"..$12.50 – 15.00
4th set "KS".......................$8.00 – 10.00
5th set "High Mount"...........$8.00 – 10.00
6th set "Ardalt" No. 6075 .$10.00 – 12.50

4th Row:
1st set "Ardalt" No. 6143.$17.50 – 20.00
2nd set "Merit"................$12.50 – 15.00
3rd set "Sango China".......$15.00 – 18.00
4th set "Ucagco"...............$15.00 – 18.00
5th set "Celebrate"............$12.50 – 15.00

5th Row:
1st set "MIOJ" (Designed by Aurger
    of Miami) ....$20.00 – 22.00
2nd set "Beteson China,"
    J. B..........................$12.50 – 15.00
3rd set "Celebrate" ....$10.00 – 12.50
4th set "MIOJ"..................$8.00 – 10.00
5th set "MIOJ"..................$8.00 – 10.00
6th set "MIOJ"..................$6.00 – 8.00

6th Row:
1st and 2nd set "MIOJ"...$10.00 – 12.50
3rd set MB in wreath ....$10.00 – 12.50
4th set "Sanjo China".........$15.00 – 18.00
5th set "MIOJ"................$15.00 – 17.50

Page 55
Top Row:
Semi-nudes plate.............$10.00 – 12.50
"Leawile China" (cup only).$15.00 – 17.50
2nd set "Ironstone Ware"..$17.50 – 20.00
3rd set "Trimont China" .....$15.00 – 18.00
4th set "Maruta China" ......$20.00 – 22.00

2nd Row:
1st set "Ucagco China"......$12.50 – 15.00
2nd set "Trimont China" .....$12.50 – 15.00
3rd set "MK" in wreath......$12.50 – 15.00
4th set "MIOJ"................$10.00 – 12.00

3rd Row:
1st set "Merit"..................$10.00 – 12.00
2nd set "MIOJ".................$8.00 – 10.00
3rd set "Aiyo China" ....$15.00 – 18.00
4th set "Gold China" ....$12.50 – 15.00

4th Row:
1st set "Merit" (leaf shaped) .$20.00 – 22.00
2nd set "Shofu China"........$17.50 – 20.00
3rd set "Saji Fancy China"..$17.50 – 20.00
4th set"MIOJ"................$10.00 – 12.00
5th and 6th "MIOJ" ....$18.00 – 20.00 ea.

5th Row:
1st and 2nd sets "Saji Fancy
    China" ....$20.00 – 22.50
3rd set "Ohashi China"......$20.00 – 22.50
4th set "MIOJ" (thatch house river
    scene) ....$15.00 – 17.50
5th set "MIOJ" (red pagoda
    scene) ....$10.00 – 12.50

6th Row:
1st set "Trimont China" ......$17.50 – 20.00
2nd set "MIOJ"................$15.00 – 17.50
3rd set "Ucagco China," "Ivory"
    pattern ....$15.00 – 17.50
4th set "Saji Fancy China".$12.50 – 15.00

Page 56
Top Row:
Demitasse, light yellow w/floral.$6.00 – 8.00
Demitasse, Oriental scene
    w/Lady........................$10.00 – 12.00
Demitasse, white w/flowers....$6.00 – 8.00
Demitasse, cream w/basket weave
    rim ....$8.00 – 10.00

Demitasse, "Moss Rose" type..$10.00 – 12.00

2nd Row:
Set, white w/pink.................$8.00 – 10.00
Set, white w/roses................$8.00 – 10.00
Set, white w/leaves...............$6.00 – 8.00
Set, fancy, footed cup
    w/daisy......................$10.00 – 12.00

3rd Row:
Demitasse, black w/lacy
    flower ....$12.50 – 15.00
Demitasse, fancy w/gold,
    2⅝".........................$17.50 – 20.00
Demitasse, hexagonal........$15.00 – 17.50
Demitasse, small dragon...$12.50 —15.00
Demitasse, large dragon....$18.00 – 20.00

4th Row:
Demitasse, green stripe .....$15.00 – 17.50
Demitasse, Colonial scene .$20.00 – 22.50
Demitasse, black and orange
    floral ....$12.50 – 15.00
Demitasse, Oriental house
    scene ....$5.00 – 6.00
Demitasse, wine rim..............$6.00 – 8.00

5th Row:
Demitasse, rust swirl.........$12.50 – 15.00
Demitasse, blue rim...............$6.00 – 8.00
Demitasse, orange luster rim .$6.00 – 8.00
Demitasse, rose w/gold ....$6.00 – 8.00
Demitasse, rust, tapered top.$12.50 – 15.00

Page 57
Top Row:
Set, floral demi ....$8.00 – 10.00
Set, white floral demi ....$10.00 – 12.00
Set, rose on tri-footed cup .$15.00 – 17.50
Set, white floral ....$8.00 – 10.00
Set, white floral ....$10.00 – 12.00

2nd Row:
Set, rust floral...................$10.00 – 12.50
Set, blue floral rim ....$10.00 – 12.00
Set, green floral rim..........$10.00 – 12.50
Set, footed, black w/gold...$17.50 – 20.00

3rd Row:
Demi Set, black and white w/gold
    design......................$15.00 – 18.00
2nd – 5th, Sets, same as above only marked
    "No 6120 Ardalt".........$15.00 – 18.00 ea.

4th Row:
Set, "Phoenix Bird," demi ..$22.50 – 25.00
Set, yellow interior............$12.50 – 15.00
Set, white demi floral ....$8.00 – 10.00
4th and 5th Sets, marked as in third
    row ....$15.00 – 18.00 ea.

5th Row:
Set, dark green swirl demi.$22.50 – 25.00
Set, yellow demi ....$10.00 – 12.50
Set (Japan only)..................$5.00 – 6.00
Set, "Royal Sealy"............$12.50 – 15.00

Set, white floral swirled
    design.......................$15.00 – 18.00

Page 58
Top Row:
Cup (Saucer?) ....$6.00 – 8.00
Demi/Set...........................$12.50 – 15.00
Cherry China Sets ....$8.00 – 12.00
Hexagonal Demitasse Set .$12.00 – 14.00

2nd Row:
1st and 4th Sets ....$7.50 – 10.00
2nd and 5th Demitasse Sets.$10.00 – 12.00
Middle Set ....$17.50 – 20.00

3rd Row:
1st and 2nd Sets ....$10.00 – 12.00
3rd and 4th Sets ....$15.00 – 17.50
5th Cup only ....$12.50 – 15.00

4th Row:
1st Demitasse Set.............$15.00 – 18.00
2nd and 4th Sets ....$10.00 – 12.00
Middle Set ....$18.00 – 20.00
5th Demitasse Set ....$6.00 – 8.00

5th Row:
1st Set............................$12.00 – 15.00
2nd and 4th Sets ....$12.00 – 15.00
Middle Set ....$20.00 – 25.00
5th Set, Souvenir Santa Claus,
    Ind............................$12.50 – 15.00

Page 59
Top Row:
1st set "OJ"......................$12.50 – 15.00
2nd set "Ucagco China" ....$10.00 – 12.50
3rd set "OJ," "W" in wreath .$15.00 – 17.50
4th set ....$12.50 – 15.00

2nd Row:
1st set "Ucagco China"......$15.00 – 18.00
2nd set "Ucagco China" ....$15.00 – 18.00
3rd set (red)....................$12.50 – 15.00
4th set (red) ....$12.50 – 15.00

3rd Row:
1st set (red) ....$10.00 – 12.50
2nd set (red) ....$10.00 – 12.50
3rd set (red)....................$12.50 – 15.00
4th set "Ucagco China" .....$15.00 – 18.00

4th Row:
1st set "OJ"......................$12.50 – 15.00
2nd set (orange)...............$10.00 – 15.00
3rd set "Trimont China" .....$17.50 – 20.00
4th set "Meito Norleans China,"
    "Livonia" ....$12.50 – 15.00

5th Row:
1st set "Merit," "OJ".........$12.50 – 15.00
2nd set (orange)...............$10.00 – 12.50
3rd set "Ucagco China".....$15.00 – 17.50
4th set (blue) ....$8.00 – 10.00

Page 60 top
Top Row:
Demitasse, 1½", violet flowers.$8.00 – 10.00

Miniature, 1", souvenir Army Navy
    Hospital ....$6.00 – 8.00
Miniature, white floral........$10.00 – 12.00
Miniature, square footed cup.$10.00 – 12.00
Miniature, scalloped, six
    sided............................$10.00 – 12.00

2nd Row:
Miniature, pink blush.........$12.50 – 15.00
Miniature, square floral
    saucer ....$5.00 – 6.00
Same as 2nd in Row 3 except blue rim and
    not souvenir ....$4.00 – 5.00
Miniature, souvenir N.Y.C. and Statue
    of Liberty ....$8.00 – 10.00
Miniature, green rim floral .....$6.00 – 8.00

3rd Row:
Miniature, blue rim, ⅞" ....$8.00 – 10.00
Miniature, green rim ....$6.00 – 8.00
Miniature, square footed
    cup ....$8.00 – 10.00
Miniature, gold/white ....$6.00 – 8.00
Demitasse, "New Orleans, La.,
    Courtyard".......................$8.00 – 10.00

Page 60 bottom
Top Row:
Set, swirled white w/flower..$8.00 – 10.00
Set, brown rim w/floral ....$6.00 – 8.00
Set, demi set floral..................$6.00 – 8.00
Set, demi "luster" w/floral ......$6.00 – 8.00
Set, demi six-sided black/red/
    white ....$12.50 – 15.00

2nd Row:
Set, demi black floral...........$8.00 – 10.00
Sets, pagoda scene and green w/gold
    decoration ....$7.50 – 10.00 ea.
Set, white w/gold souvenir.....$6.00 – 8.00
Set, pink floral ....$6.00 – 8.00
Set, blue w/scalloped rim ......$6.00 – 8.00

3rd Row:
St. Denis size, 3", floral .....$10.00 – 12.50
St. Denis size, basket,
    decorated ....$8.00 – 10.00
Set, "Mother," 4⅛"............$25.00 – 30.00
Cup, "Mother," decorated floral..$20.00 – 22.50

Page 61 top
Top Row:
Set, blue rim floral ....$8.00 – 10.00
Set, red rim floral ....$8.00 – 10.00
Set, w/emblem....................$10.00 – 12.50
Set, w/house scene............$10.00 – 12.50

2nd Row:
Set, gold rimmed floral ....$8.00 – 10.00
Set, w/fancy M ....$8.00 – 10.00
Set, w/pagoda scene.........$12.50 – 15.00
Set, elephant head over A
    emblem...........................$8.00 – 10.00

3rd Row:
Set, blue w/floral ....$12.50 – 15.00

Price Guide →

Set, LEDA in gold on side .$15.00 – 17.50
Set, white floral ....$12.50 – 15.00
Set, floral w/fancy handle..$15.00 – 18.00

Page 61 bottom

Top Row:
Set, floral ....$8.00 – 10.00
Set, w/emblem.................$10.00 – 12.50
Set, floral w/blue "luster" rim .$10.00 – 12.00
Set, floral ....$12.50 – 15.00

2nd Row:
Set "Phoenix Bird" ....$22.50 – 25.00
Set, rust rimmed, floral ......$10.00 – 12.00
Set, floral w/stripe..............$8.00 – 10.00
Set, floral w/blue "luster" rim..$8.00 – 10.00

3rd Row:
Set, tulip design...............$10.00 – 12.50
Set, pink rimmed..............$10.00 – 12.00
Set, floral ribbed..............$15.00 – 17.50
Set, blue rimmed, floral
   interior ....$12.50 – 15.00

Page 62

Top Row:
1st and 5th Sets,
   Hexagonal ....$15.00 – 17.50 ea.
2nd Set ....$7.50 – 9.00
3rd and 4th Sets ....$7.00 – 8.50 ea.

2nd Row:
1st, Cup Only....................$8.00 – 10.00
2nd Set ....$12.50 – 15.00
3rd Set............................$15.00 – 18.00
4th (Satsuma) Set.............$22.50 – 25.00
5th Dragon Set.................$17.50 – 20.00

3rd Row:
1st, 3rd, 4th Sets..............$10.00 – 12.50 ea.
2nd Set, Flower Petal ....$20.00 – 25.00
5th Set, Blue Willow..........$12.00 – 15.00

4th Row:
1st, 4th, 5th Sets ....$12.50 – 15.00 ea.
2nd, 3rd Sets ....$17.50 – 20.00 ea.

Page 63

Top Row:
1st, Cabin Scene w/Five Chickens..$17.50 – 20.00
2nd and 3rd, Plums or Cherries..$20.00 – 25.00 ea.
4th, Sailing Ship...............$17.50 – 20.00

2nd Row:
Fish Dish ....$12.50 – 15.00
Lake Scene w/Two Buildings..$6.00 – 8.00
Floral Handled Relish...........$6.00 – 8.00
Lake Scene w/Two Swans.$10.00 – 12.50
Birds of Paradise w/Luster
   Edge ....$12.50 – 15.00

3rd Row:
Geisha Girl Plates............$20.00 – 25.00 ea.

4th Row:
Brown Leaf w/Handle........$8.00 – 10.00
Brown, Curled Finger Handle..$8.00 – 10.00

Brown Divided Dish ....$5.00 – 6.00
Brown w/Grapes and Four Holes for
   Handles ....$6.00 – 8.00

Page 64

Top Row:
Plate, 7" ....$25.00 – 35.00
Plate, 6" ....$20.00 – 25.00
Lattice Plate, 6" ....$25.00 – 30.00
Fruit Plate ....$20.00 – 22.50

2nd Row:
Candy or Relish, 5½" ....$6.00 – 8.00
Handled Plate, 4¼"............$8.00 – 10.00
Handled Plate, 4¼"............$8.00 – 10.00
4th and 5th, Floral Plates,
   4½".............................$10.00 – 12.00 ea.

3rd Row:
1st – 3rd, Floral Bowls,
   5½"..............................$10.00 – 12.50 ea.
4th, Lattice-edge Floral Plate.$10.00 – 12.50
5th, Lattice-edge Fruit Bowl,
   5½"..............................$15.00 – 17.50

4th Row:
Brown Tri-Plate ....$10.00 – 12.50
Brown Leaf-Shaped Plate ..$8.00 – 10.00
Brown Floral Plate, Brown
   Bowl ....$5.00 – 6.00 ea.
Brown Cloverleaf-Shaped
   Plate..............................$8.00 – 10.00

Page 65

Top Row:
Cup and Saucer Wall Plaque
   3¼"...............................$7.50 – 9.00
Flower Bowl, "Pico" ....$8.00 – 10.00
Snack Plate, 9" leaf, "Shofu
   China" ....$8.00 – 10.00
Match Safe, 6¼" ....$35.00 – 37.50

2nd Row:
Plate, 5" ....$6.00 – 7.50
Plate, 4½", Ardalt................$7.50 – 9.00
Children's Vases, 2" pr. .....$15.00 – 20.00

3rd Row:
Bowl, 7" ....$15.00 – 18.00
Plate, 6⅜", "Shozan".........$10.00 – 12.50
Hanging Planter w/24" pottery chain,
   "Marumon" ....$50.00 – 65.00

4th Row:
Bowl, 5¾" "Ucagco"............$8.00 – 10.00
Handled Leaf Plate, 5½"...$10.00 – 12.50
Handled Plate, 5¾"..........$12.50 – 15.00

Page 66

Top Row:
Yellow Flower....................$12.50 – 15.00
Scalloped Edge Fruit w/Peach and
   Plums............................$7.50 – 10.00
Purple Leaf.........................$6.00 – 8.00
Orange Flowers ....$15.00 – 18.00
Oval Lattice Bowl ....$12.50 – 15.00

2nd Row:
Rose Floral Dish ....$4.00 – 5.00
"Cup of Gold" ....$10.00 – 12.50
Lattice Ladies w/Child......$17.50 – 20.00
Shell w/Couple ....$6.00 – 8.00
Blue Edge Floral...............$8.00 – 10.00
Red Edge Floral ....$8.00 – 10.00

3rd Row:
Floral.................................$2.50 – 4.00
Leaf Relish.......................$10.00 – 12.50
Latticed Floral Bowl.............$6.00 – 8.00
Floral Leaf..........................$7.50 – 10.00
Tree Scene........................$5.00 – 6.00
Dog ....$12.50 – 15.00
Latticed Fruit w/Grapes and
   Peach............................$8.00 – 10.00

4th Row:
Floral Leaf ....$2.50 – 4.00
Latticed Floral......................$6.00 – 8.00
Latticed Fruit and Flowers..$12.50 – 15.00
Square Floral Bowl.............$6.00 – 8.00
Square, Handled Floral Plate.$8.00 – 10.00
Square, Handled Floral Plate.$8.00 – 10.00

Page 67

Top Row:
1st and 5th, Small Leaf, 2½"..$3.00 – 4.00 ea.
2nd – 4th, Fruit Plates, 6" .$12.50 – 15.00 ea.

2nd Row:
Palette, signed "V. Soga"...$12.50 – 15.00
Palette, signed "K. Ohi".....$12.50 – 15.00
Oval, 7½" Latticed-edged
   Bowl..............................$20.00 – 22.50
Bowl, 4½", Lattice Edge...$15.00 – 17.50

3rd Row:
1st, Maple Leaf....................$3.00 – 4.00
2nd, Dog Plate, 2¾"...........$8.00 – 10.00
3rd and 5th, Small Flower
   Plate................................$2.00 – 3.00 ea.
4th, Leaf w/Bee ....$5.00 – 6.00
6th, Tray w/Translation ....$8.00 – 10.00
7th, Embossed Rose on Tray ..$4.00 – 5.00

4th Row:
1st, Fish on Shell-Shaped Tray.$8.00 – 10.00
2nd and 5th, Scenic Plates....$2.50 – 4.00 ea.
3rd and 4th, Scenic Plates ....$4.00 – 5.00 ea.
6th, Clover Scene...............$8.00 – 10.00
7th, Sea Shell, 3" ....$2.50 – 4.00

5th Row:
Handled Floral Bowl ....$12.50 – 15.00
Sea Shell, 4" ....$5.00 – 6.00
Handled "Luster" Bowl......$10.00 – 12.00
Handled Plate, 4¼"..............$6.00 – 8.00
Handled Plate, 4¼"..............$6.00 – 8.00

Page 68

Top Row:
Plate "Noritake" ....$10.00 – 12.00

2nd Row:
Hexagonal Plate.................$3.00 – 3.50

248

2nd and 4th Plates ....$3.00 – 4.00
3rd Plate ....$10.00 – 12.50
5th Plate...........................$2.50 – 3.00

3rd Row:
Plate, Souvenir of Oklahoma City,
    Okla. ....$4.00 – 5.00
2nd Plate w/Sailboat...........$8.00 – 10.00
Ohio Map......................$15.00 – 17.50
Celery ....$6.00 – 8.00

4th Row:
Violet Plate....................$20.00 – 25.00
Fruit Plate ....$15.00 – 18.00
Flower Plate...................$10.00 – 12.50

Bottom:
1st Plate ....$2.50 – 3.00
Bonbon Tray ....$8.50 – 10.00
Flower Plate....................$8.00 – 10.00

Page 69
Top Row:
Plates, 8¼", "Rosetti" ....$22.50 – 25.00 ea.
"Cup of Gold," "Hibiscus," "Hybrid Cattelya"

2nd Row:
Handled Divided Tray, 10", Elephant
    head mark ....$10.00 – 12.50
2nd and 3rd Plates, 3¼",
    souvenir ....$5.00 – 6.00 ea.
4th Plate, 3⅜", souvenir........$5.00 – 6.00
Flower Frog w/seven holes,
    4½"...............................$10.00 – 12.50

3rd Row:
Bowl, 6" ....$12.50 – 15.00
Plate, 7¾", "Ardalt" ....$25.00 – 30.00
Plate, 8" ....$65.00 – 75.00
Bowl, 6" ....$12.50 – 15.00

4th Row:
Leaf, 6½", "Ucagco China" .$8.00 – 10.00
Leaf, 3", "Kyokuto China"......$4.00 – 5.00
Leaf, 5½", "Chubu China" .$10.00 – 12.50

5th Row:
Plates, 6⅛", "SGK China,"
    "Andrea" ....$20.00 – 25.00 ea.

Page 70
Top Row:
Celluloid Reindeer, 7" x 7½" .$12.50 – 15.00
Santa Planter, 5½" x 6".....$27.50 – 30.00
Tree, w/Bulbs, 6¼ ....$7.50 – 10.00

2nd Row:
Skier, 3½" ....$25.00 – 30.00
2nd, 3rd, and 4th Ornaments,
    3½" ....$6.00 – 7.50
Holly Leaf, 4" w/wire
    attachments...................$3.00 – 3.50 ea.
Santa Pipe Cleaner, 4" .....$20.00 – 22.50
Santa Ornament, 4" ....$25.00 – 30.00

3rd Row:
Nativity Set, 7 piece, 2½" .$40.00 – 45.00

4th and 5th Rows:
Nativity Set in papier-maché
    (missing Christ Child) .$125.00 – 150.00 set

Page 71
Column 1: (vertically)
Box of 12 Bells, "MIOJ" on box
    No. 51.........................$30.00 – 35.00
Box of 12 Ornaments, each 3¼"
    long ....$35.00 – 40.00

Column 2:
Box of 12 Ornaments, each 3¼" long,
    "MIOJ" ....$35.00 – 40.00
Box of 12 various designs, each 2" long,
    "MIOJ" ....$20.00 – 25.00
"Christmas Tree Ornaments,"
    1 Doz. ....$12.50 – 15.00
"Glass Ball Ornaments," 1 Doz.,
    Maker "MIOJ" ....$12.50 – 15.00

Page 72 top
Top Row:
Cuckoo Clock, 5"..............$12.50 – 15.00
Christmas Ball Tree ....$8.00 – 10.00
Christmas Ornaments........$20.00 – 25.00
Santas, red papier-maché and blue
    w/silver hat...................$40.00 – 50.00 ea.

2nd Row:
Tree Ornaments ....$10.00 – 12.50 ea.

Page 72 bottom
Top Row:
Ship..................................$7.50 – 9.00
Blooming Flower ....$4.00 – 5.00
Frog Hanger ....$17.50 – 20.00
Man Hanger......................$15.00 – 17.50
Mermaid..........................$15.00 – 17.50
Floating Water Lily ....$8.50 – 10.00

Bottom Row:
Arches ....$10.00 – 12.50 ea.

Page 73
Top Row:
Ship.................................$9.00 – 10.00
Bisque Boy and Girl ....$17.50 – 22.50
Castle.............................$10.00 – 12.00
Bisque Boy ....$15.00 – 17.50

2nd Row:
Castle................................$6.00 – 8.00
Cats ....$20.00 – 22.00
Goldfish ....$8.00 – 10.00
Bisque Boy and Girl ....$12.50 – 15.00

Bottom Row:
Castle atop Bridge ....$10.00 – 12.00
Pagoda Bridge ....$10.00 – 12.00
Mermaid..........................$20.00 – 22.00

Page 74
Top Row:
Lorelei Bud Vase................$8.00 – 10.00
Lorelei Planter ....$12.50 – 15.00
Lorelei w/Cello...................$8.00 – 10.00

Lorelei Bud Vase................$8.00 – 10.00
5th – 7th, Lorelei ....$8.00 – 10.00 ea.

2nd Row:
Orange-tail Mermaid on
    Rocks ....$20.00 – 25.00
Blue-tail Mermaid on Rocks.$20.00 – 25.00
Same as 2nd only unpainted.$17.50 – 20.00
Bisque, 3½", orange tail ....$20.00 – 22.50
5th and 6th, Lorelei Bud
    Vases...........................$8.00 – 10.00 ea.

3rd Row:
1st and 2nd, Same as 4th in second
    row ....$20.00 – 25.00 ea.
3rd, Mermaid Holding Blue
    Tail ....$20.00 – 25.00
4th, Mermaid Sitting w/Orange
    Tail ....$20.00 – 25.00
5th, Mermaid w/Small Blue-tipped
    Tail ....$20.00 – 22.50
6th and 7th, Reclining Mermaids,
    4⅜".............................$25.00 – 30.00 ea.

4th Row:
1st and 3rd, Fish Bowl
    Pagodas ....$10.00 – 12.00 ea.
2nd and 4th, Mermaid
    Sitters.........................$17.50 – 20.00 ea.
5th, Mermaid on Shell ....$20.00 – 25.00
6th, Pagoda ....$8.00 – 10.00

5th Row:
1st, 4th, and 5th, Fish Bowl
    Pagodas ....$10.00 – 12.00 ea.
2nd and 3rd, Fish Bowl
    Pagodas ....$10.00 – 12.00 ea.

Page 75
Top Row:
"Wedgwood"-style Pitcher,
    2⅝"...............................$8.00 – 10.00
"Wedgwood"-style Pitcher ..$10.00 – 12.50
"Wedgwood"-style Pitcher,
    4¼"...............................$17.50 – 20.00
Floral Pitcher ....$10.00 – 12.50
Floral Pitcher ....$12.50 – 15.00
Narrow Neck Embossed Flower
    Pitcher...........................$7.50 – 10.00
Pitcher..................................$5.00 – 6.00

2nd Row:
Basket................................$6.00 – 8.00
Basket................................$5.00 – 6.00
Blue Wicker Basket ....$6.00 – 8.00
Wishing Well ....$10.00 – 12.50
Basket w/Embossed Flower..$4.00 – 5.00
Lady w/Two Baskets ....$45.00 – 50.00

3rd Row:
Wheelbarrow w/Roses,
    1⅝" x 5".........................$8.00 – 10.00
Wheelbarrow w/Cherry........$6.00 – 8.00
Wheelbarrow w/Yellow Flower.$4.00 – 5.00
Blue Wheelbarrow................$4.00 – 5.00
White Wheelbarrow.............$2.50 – 4.00

Price Guide →

4th Row:

1st – 3rd, Suitcase, 2" ....$4.00 – 5.00 ea.
4th, Basket w/Grapes.........$8.00 – 10.00
5th, Basket w/Roses ....$6.00 – 8.00
6th, Bird handled Basket ....$8.00 – 10.00

5th Row:

Blue Basket, 2" ....$3.50 – 5.00
Open Teapot........................$2.50 – 4.00
Coffee Pot w/Lid.................$8.00 – 10.00
Teapot w/Lid.......................$8.00 – 10.00
Blue Coffee Pot w/Lid ....$8.00 – 10.00
Teapot w/Lid, embossed rose$8.00 – 10.00
Teapot w/Lid.......................$8.00 – 10.00

Page 76

Top Row:

All Items Save 2nd Teapot ..$5.00 – 7.00
2nd Teapot w/Removable Lid .$6.00 – 8.00

2nd Row:

All Items Save Half Potty and Lookout
  Mt. Pitcher ....$3.50 – 4.00
Half Potty...........................$3.00 – 3.50
Lookout Mt. Pitcher.............$4.00 – 5.00

3rd Row:

All Items Save Martha/George and
  Floral Vase ....$3.00 – 3.50
Martha and George Set....$15.00 – 17.50
Blue Floral Vase..................$8.00 – 10.00

4th Row:

All Items ....$4.00 – 5.00

5th Row:

All Items Save Small Trays and Nude
  Boy ....$3.50 – 4.00
Nude Boy ....$4.50 – 5.00
Tray w/6 Pieces—Only the trays are marked
  "Made in Occupied Japan" Removable Lid
  on Pitcher .....$17.50 – 20.00 (complete)
  Incomplete ....$2.00 each piece

Page 77

Top Row:

1st, Pitcher w/Yellow Flower,
  3⅛"...................................$3.00 – 4.00
2nd and 4th, Pitchers w/Brown
  Design ....$3.00 – 4.00 ea.
3rd, Floral Pitcher.................$4.00 – 5.00
5th, Pitcher, 5⅛".................$6.00 – 8.00
6th, Green Pitcher w/Orange
  Flower ....$5.00 – 6.00
7th, Blue Pitcher w/Draped
  Lady.................................$8.00 – 10.00
8th, Pitcher w/Basket Weave
  Design ....$3.00 – 4.00

2nd Row:

1st, Ornate Water Can, 3"..$10.00 – 12.00
2nd, White Can w/Raised Pink
  Rose ....$6.00 – 8.00
3rd and 4th, White w/Red Rose or
  Basket Weave ....$4.00 – 5.00 ea.
5th, Floral Can....................$2.00 – 3.00

6th, Yellow Can w/Raised
  Rose ....$6.00 – 8.00
7th, Blue Can w/Raised Pink
  Rose ....$6.00 – 8.00

3rd Row:

1st and 12th, Coffee Pots, 2".$4.00 – 5.00 ea.
2nd – 6th, 10th, Pitchers ......$3.00 – 4.00 ea.
7th – 9th, Water Cans ....$2.50 – 3.50 ea.
11th, Pitcher.......................$3.00 – 4.00

4th Row:

1st, Pitcher, 2⅜"................$3.00 – 4.00
2nd, Ornate Handle Pitcher ..$6.00 – 8.00
3rd, Small Pitcher, 1¾".........$3.00 – 4.00
4th, White Pitcher w/White Raised
  Rose ....$3.00 – 4.00
5th and 6th, Matching Urns,
  3⅛".................................$3.00 – 4.00 ea.
7th, White Pitcher w/Pink Rose.$3.00 – 4.00
8th and 9th, Pitchers w/Raised
  Roses ....$6.00 – 8.00 ea.
10th, Bird Pitcher.............$10.00 – 12.50

5th Row:

Water Can, 1¾"...................$2.00 – 3.50
White Floral Pitcher ....$3.00 – 4.00
Blue Pitcher ....$3.00 – 4.00
Pitcher................................$3.00 – 4.00
White Teapot w/Lid ....$5.00 – 6.00
Coffee Pot w/Raised Flower and
  Lid..................................$10.00 – 12.00
Teapot, decorated like Coffee
  Pot ....$6.00 – 8.00
Round Teakettle w/Lid..........$6.00 – 8.00
Coffee Pot w/Lid..................$6.00 – 8.00

Page 78

Top Row:

Outhouse w/Black Figures .$30.00 – 40.00
Blue Pitchers.......................$4.00 – 5.00 ea.
Clocks ....$6.00 – 7.50 ea.
Grandfather Clock ....$9.00 – 11.00

2nd Row:

Blue Teakettle (Lid Lifts).......$6.00 – 8.00
Souvenir Pitchers ....$3.00 – 4.00 ea.
Other Items ....$3.00 – 4.00 ea.

3rd Row:

Shoes (Note the cat heads on
  two.) ....$6.00 – 8.00 ea.

4th Row:

1st, 4th, 5th, Shoes..............$4.00 – 5.00 ea.
2nd Bisque Shoe.............$10.00 – 12.00
3rd Shoe, Outdoor Scene .$12.00 – 15.00

5th Row:

Egg Cups......................$12.00 – 15.00 ea.
Piano (2 Part)....................$8.00 – 10.00
Dutch Clog Shoe Planter ......$6.00 – 8.00
Bench................................$3.00 – 4.00

6th Row:

Stroller, Soldiers, Bootee ......$5.00 – 6.00 ea.

Covered Wagon ....$5.00 – 7.00
Heart Box ....$10.00 – 12.00
Cinderella Coach and
  Horses ....$10.00 – 12.50

Page 79

Top Row:

Rust Shoe w/Embossed Flower,
  2⅜"................................$8.00 – 10.00
Blue Boot, 3½"...................$4.00 – 5.00
Cowboy Boot, 4⅜"..............$6.00 – 8.00
Boot, 6½"......................$10.00 – 12.50
Tulip Boot...........................$6.00 – 8.00
Pink Baby Boot....................$4.00 – 5.00
George Washington Shoe..$10.00 – 12.50
Ruffled Embossed Flower
  Shoe..............................$18.00 – 20.00

2nd Row:

1st and 2nd, White Shoes w/Flowers,
  1¾"................................$3.00 – 4.00 ea.
3rd, Show w/Rabbit, 2⅜"......$6.00 – 8.00
4th, Dutch Boy w/Shoe ....$8.00 – 10.00
5th, Lady w/Children on Embossed Floral
  Shoe, 5" h ....$75.00 – 85.00
6th, Blue Floral Shoe ....$6.00 – 8.00
7th, Baby Shoe ....$4.00 – 5.00
8th, White Shoe ....$3.00 – 4.00
9th, Blue Embossed Floral Shoe,
  3½"................................$8.00 – 10.00

3rd Row:

1st, Souvenir Ky. Dam, Ky. ...$6.00 – 8.00
2nd, Man's Shoe ....$3.00 – 4.00
3rd, Lady's Shoe...................$3.00 – 4.00
4th and 6th, Baby Bootee
  Planters ....$5.00 – 6.00 ea.
5th, Rabbit Shoes ....$8.00 – 10.00
7th, 9th, and 10th, White or Black
  Shoes ....$3.00 – 4.00 ea.
8th, Brown Floral Shoe ....$8.00 – 10.00

4th Row:

1st and 3rd, Heeled Shoe,
  1¼"................................$3.00 – 4.00 ea.
2nd, Boot ....$3.00 – 4.00
4th, White w/Flowers ....$4.00 – 5.00
5th, Blue w/Pink Flower.......$3.00 – 4.00
6th, 7th, 9th, and 11th,
  Baskets ....$4.00 – 5.00 ea.
8th, Urn.............................$3.00 – 4.00
10th, Urn w/Fruit ....$5.00 – 6.00
12th, Shoe..........................$3.00 – 4.00

5th Row:

1st, 2nd, 6th – 8th, 11th,
  Baskets ....$4.00 – 5.00 ea.
3rd and 10th, Wreaths and Handle
  w/Rose ....$3.00 – 4.00 ea.
5th, Cat w/Basket.................$6.00 – 8.00
9th, Small Basket..................$2.00 – 3.00
12th, Shoe w/Heel................$2.00 – 3.00
13th, Ruffled Shoe................$4.00 – 5.00

Page 80

Top Row (Blue Willow)

Cereal Bowl, 5¾"..............$12.50 – 15.00

Sugar w/Lid.....................$17.50 – 20.00
Creamer ....$12.50 – 15.00
Berry Bowl, 4¾" ....$10.00 – 12.50

2nd Row:
Cup and Saucer...............$17.50 – 20.00
Salad Plate, 7" ....$8.00 – 10.00
Dinner Plate, 9" ....$12.50 – 15.00

3rd Row:
Demitasse Cup and Saucer..$20.00 – 22.00
Cup and Saucer...............$15.00 – 17.50
Demitasse Saucer ....$4.00 – 5.00
Cup and Saucer...............$17.50 – 20.00

Page 81
Top Row (Blue Willow)
Saucer ....$2.00 – 3.00
Dinner Plate, 9" ....$12.50 – 15.00
Sugar w/Lid.....................$17.50 – 20.00
Salad Plate, 7" ....$8.00 – 10.00
Creamer ....$12.50 – 15.00
Cereal Bowl, 5¾"............$12.50 – 15.00
Berry Bowl, 4½" ....$10.00 – 12.50

2nd Row:
Dinner Plate, w/red and yellow
   flowers........................$17.50 – 20.00
Berry Bowl, same ....$10.00 – 12.50
Bread and Butter.................$4.00 – 5.00
Dinner Plate ....$12.50 – 15.00
Saucer ....$2.00 – 3.00

3rd Row:
Cup and Saucer...............$17.50 – 20.00
Platter, 12" ....$40.00 – 50.00
Berry Bowl ....$10.00 – 12.50
Platter, 12" ....$30.00 – 35.00

Page 82
Top Row:
Plate, 10", "Empire Shape, Meito China,
   Ivory China" ....$10.00 – 12.50
Demitasse Cup and Saucer,
   "Highmount" ....$8.00 – 10.00
Plate, 7½", "Hira China" ....$6.00 – 8.00
Plate, 10", "Empire Shape, Meito China,
   Dexter, Ivory China".....$10.00 – 12.50
Cup, "Merit China" ....$8.00 – 10.00

2nd Row:
Demitasse Cup and Saucer.$8.00 – 10.00
"Blue Willow" Cup and
   Saucer ....$17.50 – 20.00
"Blue Willow" Bowl, 5", ...$10.00 – 12.50
"Blue Willow" Egg Cup, 3¾"..$22.50 – 25.00

3rd Row:
Plate, 5⅝", marked K in
   circle ....$10.00 – 12.00
Demitasse Cup and Saucer, "Ucagco
   China" ....$10.00 – 12.00
Plate, 7½" (same as 1st)....$12.50 – 15.00
Sugar (same as 1st).........$12.50 w/o
   lid, 17.50 – 20.00 w/lid

4th Row:
Platter, 10" x 14", "Ironstone
   Ware"............................$30.00 – 35.00

"Blue Willow" Child's Tureen,
   5" x 2¾".......................$50.00 – 60.00

Dinnerware Sets
Ash Tray.......................$8.00 – 10.00
Bowl, berry, 4" to 4⅞".......$8.00 – 10.00
Bowl, cereal, 5" to 6½"......$12.00 – 15.00
Bowl, soup, 7" to 9"........$15.00 – 20.00
Bow, round vegetable, 9½" to
   10½"...........................$35.00 – 45.00
Bowl, oval vegetable, 10" to
   12".............................$40.00 – 50.00
Casserole, covered...........$65.00 – 85.00
Comport or Compote ....$22.50 – 25.00
Creamer ....$15.00 – 17.50
Cup ....$8.00 – 15.00
Cup, Demitasse ....$12.00 – 15.00
Gravy ....$15.00 – 20.00
Gravy Platter ....$10.00 – 15.00
Gravy w/Attached Platter.$30.00 – 50.00
Plate, bread and butter 5¾" to
   6¾".............................$4.00 – 6.00
Plate, salad, 7" to 8"............$6.00 – 8.00
Plate, dinner, 9" to 11".....$15.00 – 20.00
Platter, small oval, 9½" to 11"..$20.00 – 30.00
Platter, medium oval, 12" to
   15".............................$35.00 – 50.00
Platter, large turkey, 16" to
   19".............................$70.00 – 95.00
Saucer ....$1.00 – 3.00
Saucer, Demitasse ....$4.00 – 5.00
Sugar w/Cover ....$20.00 – 30.00
Teapot.........................$100.00 – 110.00

Set for 4 including cups, saucers, plates in 3
   sizes, cereal and soup bowls, creamer and
   covered sugar ....$175.00 – 200.00
Set for 6 including all items listed for service for 4
   and gravy boat and platter.$225.00 – 250.00
Set for 8 including all of service for 6 and
   small platter ....$275.00 – 350.00
Set for 12 including all of service for 4 with 3
   platters and serving bowls .$400.00 – 500.00

Page 83
Handcrafted, "Iris"
Handcrafted, "Bamboo"

Page 84
Kent China, "Orange Blossom"

Page 85
Yamaka China, no name

Page 86
Noritake China, M in wreath mark, no name

Page 87
Meito Norleans China, "Livonia," called "Dog-
wood" by collectors

Page 88
Grace China, "Rochelle"

Page 89
Aladdin Fine China, "Forget-Me-Not"

Page 90
Cherry China, no pattern name

Page 91
Diamond China, no pattern name

Page 92
Sango China, no pattern name

Page 93
Ucago China, no pattern name, apples or
crabapples

Page 94
Aladdin Fine China, "Garland"

Page 95
Row 1 and Row 2 are "Wild Rose China"
Tea Set (Teapot, Creamer, Sugar & Lid, 4
   Cups & Saucers........$200.00 – 250.00 set
Dinnerware Set for Eight .$400.00 – 500.00

Row 3 and Row 4 are "Noritake"
Demitasse Set ....$250.00 – 300.00 set

Page 96
Top Row:
1st and 3rd, Ucagco China, w/emblem in gold,
   (yellow flower pattern)
4th, Regal China, Emerald pattern w/crown
   emblem
5th, Yamaka China, (bamboo-like pattern)

2nd Row:
   Left: Noritake China
   Right: Norumi China, Magnolia pattern

3rd Row:
Left: Noritake China, M in wreath mark
Right: Red mark, gold swirl on white pattern

Page 97
Top Row:
Left: Rosetti, Spring Violets, gold mark crown
Right: Hadson Chinaware, red anchor mark,
   (ivy type pattern)

2nd Row:
Gold, Hand Painted, (floral pattern)

3rd Row:
Hadson Chinaware, red anchor mark, (yellow
   rose pattern)

Page 98
Top Row:
Green Pixies ....$17.50 – 20.00 ea.
Planter Pixie ....$15.00 – 17.50

2nd Row:
Elves Riding Insects/
   Animals ....$25.00 – 30.00 ea

3rd Row:
Mushroom Elves..............$12.50 – 15.00 ea.
Elf Astride Insect............$25.00 – 30.00

4th Row:
Pink Suited Elves.............$20.00 – 22.50 ea.

Price Guide ~

Page 99

Top Row:
One-handed Orator Gnome,
5⅛"..................$12.50 – 15.00
Tired Old Gnome.........$10.00 – 12.50
Red Elf w/Pot...................$15.00 – 17.50
Elf w/Log.......................$12.50 – 15.00
Red Elf w/Planter...........$15.00 – 17.50
Gnome w/Basket..............$12.50 – 15.00

2nd Row:
1st, Leaf Hat Recliner.......$10.00 – 12.50
2nd and 3rd, Leaf Reclining
    Pair ....$25.00 – 30.00 pr.
4th, Elf on Frog..............$25.00 – 30.00
5th, Elf on Caterpillar........$20.00 – 22.50

3rd Row:
1st – 3rd and 6th, Purple Suited
    Elves ....$15.00 – 17.50 ea.
4th and 5th, Green Suited
    Elves ....$17.50 – 20.00 ea.

4th Row:
1st and 3rd, Orange Suited
    Sitters....................$12.50 – 15.00 ea.
2nd and 4th, Purple or Blue
    Recliners ....$12.50 – 15.00 ea.
5th, Old Lady Gnome, 2½" ...$5.00 – 6.00
6th, Old Lady Gnome, 3¾" .$8.00 – 10.00
7th and 8th, Old Man
    Gnome ....$8.00 – 10.00 ea.

5th Row:
1st and 3rd, Wooden Looking
    Figurines..................$8.00 – 10.00 ea.
2nd and 4th – 8th, Wooden Looking
    Musicians ....$8.00 – 10.00.

Page 100

Top Row:
All Items Save Center Boy
    w/Duck..................$8.00 – 10.00
Boy w/Duck ....$12.50 – 15.00

2nd Row:
All Items Save Reclining Girl ..$6.00 – 8.00
Reclining Girl w/Bird ....$10.00 – 12.00

3rd Row:
All Items ....$5.00 – 6.00

4th Row:
1st Five Items ....$5.00 – 6.00
Last Five Items.................$15.00 – 20.00

5th Row:
Boy and Dog, Left ....$20.00 – 25.00
Remaining Items...............$15.00 – 20.00

Page 101

Top Row:
Boy w/Broken Sprinkler,
    4½".........................$30.00 – 35.00
Basket Girl, 5½" ....$27.50 – 30.00
Basket Boy, 5¾"...............$27.50 – 30.00
Flute-Playing Boy, 4½" .....$18.00 – 20.00

2nd Row:
Skier, 4½" ....$25.00 – 27.50
Boy w/Begging Dog, 5" ....$35.00 – 40.00
Hiker, 4" ....$15.00 – 17.50
Girl w/Basket, 4½" ....$15.00 – 17.50
Boy w/Duck, 3¾"..............$20.00 – 25.00

3rd Row:
1st and 3rd pr., 5½" (probably
    bookends) $35.00 ea./ .....$75.00 – 80.00 pr.
Umbrella, pair, 6" ....$35.00 – 40.00

4th Row:
1st and 3rd Tyrolean pair,
    5"....................$40.00 – 45.00 ea.
Gardening pair, 5½"..........$50.00 – 60.00

Page 102

Top Row:
Boy and Girl (approx. 8")..$40.00 – 45.00 ea.
    Pair ....$90.00 – 95.00

2nd Row:
Girl and Doll....................$40.00 – 50.00
Children with Boat............$40.00 – 50.00
Children with Umbrella ......$40.00 – 50.00

3rd Row:
Walking Boy (Larger of Two) .$20.00 – 22.50
Artist and Palette.............$40.00 – 45.00
Umbrella Boy ....$20.00 – 25.00
Walking Boy (Smaller of Two) .$12.50 – 15.00
Hiker ....$12.50 – 15.00

4th Row:
Girls with Geese................$20.00 – 25.00
Girl Feeding Geese...........$17.50 – 20.00
Girls with Baskets ....$20.00 – 25.00 ea.

Page 103

Top Row:
1st, Boy Playing Accordion ...$7.50 – 10.00
2nd, Boy Playing Bass Fiddle .$7.50 – 10.00
3rd, Boy Playing Accordion,
    5"...................................$10.00 – 12.50
4th and 5th, Girl and Boy
    Fiddlers ....$10.00 – 12.00 ea.
6th and 7th, Boy Playing
    Accordion ....$10.00 – 12.50 ea.
8th, Boy Playing Mandolin ..$10.00 – 12.50

2nd Row:
1st, Girl Playing Accordion w/Dog,
    3⅞" ....$10.00 – 12.50
2nd, Boy Playing Accordion
    w/Dog ....$10.00 – 12.50
3rd, Girl Playing Accordion ..$8.00 – 10.00
4th, Boy Playing Fiddlers......$5.00 – 6.00
5th and 6th, Boys Playing Fiddle or
    Mandolin..........................$5.00 – 6.00 ea.
7th, Boy Playing Accordion .$7.50 – 10.00
8th, Boy Playing Accordion ...$6.00 – 8.00
9th, Boy Playing Violin ....$6.00 – 8.00

3rd Row:
1st, Boy Playing Accordion,
    2⅝"...................................$3.00 – 4.00

2nd and 10th, Boy Playing
    Accordion ....$3.00 – 4.00 ea.
3rd and 4th, Girl Playing Fiddle & Boy
    Playing Accordion......................$5.00 – 6.00 ea.
5th – 9th, Musicians ....$3.00 – 4.00 ea.

4th Row:
1st, Accordion Playing for Chicken,
    4⅛"...........................$6.00 – 8.00
2nd, 3rd, and 6th, Violin Playing Fence
    Sitters.........................$6.00 – 8.00 ea.
4th and 5th, Boy Playing
    Accordion ....$6.00 – 8.00 ea.
7th, Colonial Boy Holding
    Violin ....$8.00 – 10.00
8th, Seated Guitar Player .....$5.00 – 6.00

5th Row:
1st – 3rd, Robed Accordion, Mandolin &
    Bass Players ....$17.50 – 20.00 ea.
4th, Girl w/Song Book, 5¾" .$30.00 – 35.00
5th, Boy Playing Accordion ...$8.00 – 10.00

Page 104

Top Row:
1st, 2nd, 4th, and 5th
    Children............................$8.00 – 10.00 ea.
3rd Boy and Boy with Pig .$10.00 – 12.50 ea.

2nd Row:
Girl on Fence ....$12.50 – 15.00
Girl in Cape ....$12.50 – 15.00
Girl with Geese ....$20.00 – 25.00
Girls with Baskets ....$20.00 – 25.00 ea.

3rd Row:
Musicians ....$10.00 – 12.50 ea.

4th Row:
Girl with Doll ....$10.00 – 12.50
Girl with Accordion............$8.00 – 10.00
Baby with Bee...................$20.00 – 25.00
Double Figure with Umbrella .$10.00 – 12.50
Tiny Girl in Green ....$5.00 – 6.00

Page 105

Top Row:
Boy w/Saxophone, 4⅝".......$8.00 – 10.00
Girl w/Teddy Bear, 5⅜"....$17.50 – 20.00
3rd and 4th, Goose Girls...$12.50 – 15.00 ea.
Girl w/Lamb....................$12.50 – 15.00
Boy w/Dog......................$10.00 – 12.50
Boy on Fence ....$8.00 – 10.00
Blue Boy ....$6.00 – 8.00

2nd Row:
1st – 4th, Skiers, 3½".......$10.00 – 12.50 ea.
5th and 6th, Skiers, 2⅛".....$4.00 – 5.00 ea.
7th and 8th, Girl w/Flower or
    Book...........................$4.00 – 5.00 ea.
9th, Boy on Fence w/Bird.....$5.00 – 6.00
10th, Boy w/Bike ....$8.00 – 10.00

3rd Row:
Girl w/Book/Basket, 3¾"......$6.00 – 8.00
Boy on Fence w/Basket, 4"...$6.00 – 8.00
Boy w/Satchel ....$6.00 – 8.00

Same as 2nd Boy except 3½" .$5.00 – 6.00
Boy w/Blue Bag ....$5.00 – 6.00
Boy Walker ....$5.00 – 6.00
Boy w/Dog........................$3.00 – 4.00
8th and 10th, Girl w/Book or
    Umbrella.................$5.00 – 6.00 ea.
Dutch Boy ....$6.00 – 8.00

4th Row:
Girl w/Basket, 3⅛" ....$4.00 – 5.00
2nd – 4th, Girl w/Duck and Boys
    w/Dog, 2¾" ....$3.00 – 4.00 ea.
Girl w/Doll ....$5.00 – 6.00
Girl w/Pitcher, 4" ....$6.00 – 8.00
Girl w/Curls ....$10.00 – 12.00
Girl w/Bucket...................$4.00 – 5.00
Boy w/Dog and Walking
    Stick.......................$8.00 – 10.00
Walking Boy....................$10.00 – 12.50
Boy w/Dog, 2½" ....$3.00 – 4.00

5th Row:
1st, Girl w/Doll Buggy, 2½" ..$4.00 – 5.00
2nd, Boy w/Horn................$3.00 – 4.00 ea.
3rd, Girl w/Satchel ....$3.00 – 4.00 ea.
4th, Boy w/Truck ....$4.00 – 5.00
5th – 7th, Girls w/Book or
    Horn ....$4.00 – 5.00 ea.
8th, Girl w/Chick ....$5.00 – 6.00 ea.
9th, Boy w/Pig ....$5.00 – 6.00 ea.
10th and 11th, Boy w/Dog, Horn or on
    Fence ....$6.00 – 8.00 ea.
12th and 13th, Girls on Fence .$5.00 – 6.00 ea.

Page 106
Top Row:
Boy w/Parrot, 5" ....$12.50 – 15.00
Boy w/Guitar, 4" ....$8.00 – 9.00
Boy w/Dog, 4¾" ....$10.00 – 12.50
Girl, 4" ....$8.00 – 10.00
Boy w/Horn, 3½" ....$6.00 – 8.00
Boy w/Chick, 2½" ....$4.00 – 5.00
Girl on Fence, 4" ....$8.00 – 10.00
Boxing Boy, 4½" ....$12.50 – 15.00

2nd Row:
Boy w/Cello, 5" ....$12.50 – 15.00
Accordion Girl, 4½" ....$8.00 – 10.00
Horn Player, 4" ....$10.00 – 12.50
Sax Player, 4½" ....$8.00 – 10.00
Girl w/Dog, 4¼" ....$8.00 – 10.00
Guitar Player, 4½" ....$12.50 – 15.00
Book Carrier, 4"................$8.00 – 10.00

3rd Row:
Boy w/Hat, 5" ....$8.00 – 10.00
Newsboy, 5½" ....$10.00 – 12.50
Walker, 6" ....$18.00 – 20.00
Horn Player, 9½" ....$27.50 – 30.00
Tuba Player, 5" ....$10.00 – 12.50
Musketeer, 5" ....$8.00 – 10.00
Hiker, 4" ....$10.00 – 12.50

4th Row:
Accordion Player, 4"..........$8.00 – 10.00
2nd to 6th Musicians, 2⅝" .....$6.00 – 7.50 ea.

Boy w/Dog, 4⅛" ....$12.50 – 15.00
Violin Player, 3¾" ....$10.00 – 12.50
Flutist, 4½" ....$8.00 – 10.00

Page 107
Top Row:
1st, Flutist, 6" ....$15.00 – 17.50
2nd – 4th, Boys Playing Drums, Tuba, and
    Horn, 4⅞" ....$12.50 – 15.00 ea.
5th, Seated Flutist ....$6.00 – 8.00
6th and 8th, Boys Playing Sax and
    Tuba ....$8.00 – 10.00 ea.
7th, Boy Playing Horn..........$5.00 – 6.00

2nd Row:
Tuba Players, 3½" ....$5.00 – 6.00
Child Seated on Fence ....$6.00 – 8.00
Children on Fence ....$8.00 – 10.00
Boy Playing to Dogs ....$10.00 – 12.00
Seated Player ....$6.00 – 8.00
6th – 8th, Seated Horn Players or
    Drummer.....................$3.00 – 4.00 ea.

3rd Row:
1st, 3rd & 6th, Horn Player for Dogs, Chick,
    or Goose, 2⅝" ....$3.00 – 4.00 ea.
2nd, Seated w/Bird.............$4.00 – 5.00
4th, Seated on Fence, 2⅜"....$3.00 – 4.00
5th, Girl w/Yellow Dress ....$6.00 – 8.00
7th, Girl w/Book................$6.00 – 8.00
8th, Girl w/Umbrella, 4¼" ...$8.00 – 10.00

4th Row:
1st, Seated w/Duck...........$15.00 – 17.50
2nd, and 5th, Girl on Fence or w/Umbrella
    and Dog ....$6.00 – 8.00 ea.
3rd, Seated Girl, 4¾".........$10.00 – 12.50
4th, Seated Girl (slightly smaller),
    4½" ....$10.00 – 12.50
6th, Girl w/Umbrella..............$4.00 – 5.00
7th, Seated Girl w/Watering
    Can ....$12.50 – 15.00

5th Row:
1st – 3rd, "Dolly Dimples" w/Rabbit or
    Duck..........................$10.00 – 12.50 ea.
4th, Girl Holding Doll, 4¼" $12.50 – 15.00
5th, Girl w/Cloak.................$6.00 – 8.00
6th – 8th, Girls w/Rabbit or
    Chick...........................$4.00 – 5.00 ea.
9th, Girl w/Pocket Book, 4⅛" .$8.00 – 10.00

Page 108
Top Row:
Flower Girl, 4⅝".................$15.00 – 17.50
Matching Boy w/Doll ....$15.00 – 17.50
Boy w/Briefcase ....$12.50 – 15.00
Matching Boy w/Book ......$12.50 – 15.00
5th and 6th, Boy and Girl..$25.00 – 30.00 pr.
7th and 8th, Girl w/Rabbit and Boy
    w/Dog ....$25.00 – 30.00 pr.

2nd Row:
1st and 2nd, Girl and Boy on Fence,
    4".............................$30.00 – 35.00 pr.
3rd and 4th, Boy w/Horn and Girl
    w/Satchel ....$22.50 – 25.00 pr.

5th and 6th, Boy w/Toy Horse and Girl
    w/Doll..........................$30.00 – 35.00 pr.
Boy w/Book ....$6.00 – 8.00
Boy w/Umbrella ....$6.00 – 8.00

3rd Row:
Girl w/Dog, 4⅛" ....$8.00 – 10.00
Girl w/Goose.......................$6.00 – 8.00
Boy w/Duck and Basket...$10.00 – 12.50
Boy w/Dog, 3".....................$6.00 – 8.00
Boy w/Dog, 4¼", Boy
    w/Rooster.....................$10.00 – 12.50 ea.
Boy w/Walking Stick ....$8.00 – 10.00
Girl w/Umbrella and Dog ....$8.00 – 10.00

4th Row:
Girl w/"Betty Boop" doll, 3¾" .$22.50 – 25.00
Girl w/Duck ....$4.00 – 5.00
Boy w/Bird Cage............$10.00 – 12.50
Boy on Fence w/Bird...........$6.00 – 8.00
Girl w/Basket......................$6.00 – 8.00
Girl on Fence ....$6.00 – 8.00
"Little White Riding Hood,"
    4⅛"............................$12.50 – 15.00
Boy w/Horn ....$5.00 – 6.00

5th Row:
Girl in Coat, 4⅛"................$8.00 – 10.00
2nd and 3rd, Boys, 3¾" ......$8.00 – 10.00 ea.
Girl w/Scarf........................$5.00 – 6.00
Seated Girl w/Book ....$6.00 – 8.00
Seated Girl w/Book ....$6.00 – 8.00
Reclining Boy w/Horn........$8.00 – 10.00
Nude w/Wheat Sheaf ....$8.00 – 10.00

Page 109
Top Row:
Ballerina............................$40.00 – 45.00
White Dress Dancer............$15.00 – 17.50
Pink Dress Dancer............$10.00 – 12.50
Lavender Dress Dancer....$25.00 – 30.00

Middle Row:
Girl Ballerina and Green Dress
    Dancer ....$12.50 – 15.00 ea.
Tall Girl w/Hat.................$25.00 – 30.00

Bottom Row:
All Dancers.........................$9.00 – 10.00

Page 110
Top Row:
Arms Behind Head Pose, 5" .$15.00 – 17.50
Holding Hem and Hat........$17.50 – 20.00
Ballerina with Net Dress, 5¾".$35.00 – 40.00
Holding Hem of Dress ....$9.00 – 10.00
Dancing Planter, 5½" ....$10.00 – 12.50

2nd Row:
Green Skirted, 3½" ....$10.00 – 12.50
White Skirted ....$9.00 – 10.00
Green and White Dress........$9.00 – 10.00
Ballerina.............................$15.00 – 17.50
Blue Ruffled Skirt...............$9.00 – 10.00
White Skirted w/Rust Top.....$4.00 – 5.00

3rd Row:
Ballerina, 4¾" ....$40.00 – 45.00

Price Guide →

Ballerina...........................$15.00 – 17.50
Ballerina...........................$10.00 – 12.50
Ballerina...........................$17.50 – 20.00
Ballerina w/Purple Dress..$30.00 – 35.00

4th Row:
1st, 3rd and 6th, Small Dancers,
    2½".............................$5.00 – 6.00 ea.
2nd, Pink, Holding Dress
    Hems..........................$9.00 – 10.00
4th and 5th, Orange Skirt and Blue
    Top.............................$5.00 – 6.00 ea.
7th, White w/Gold...............$6.00 – 8.00

5th Row:
1st and 6th, Yellow Skirt,
    3½"..............................$8.00 – 10.00 ea.
2nd and 5th, 5⅜"..............$20.00 – 25.00 ea.
3rd, Hands Behind Head
    Pose...........................$15.00 – 17.50
4th, Windswept Lady........$12.50 – 15.00

Page 111

Top Row:
Lady Holding Dress, 4¼"..$10.00 – 12.50
Lady Holding Hat, 5".........$12.50 – 15.00
Lady Holding Skirt............$12.50 – 15.00
Lady in Curtsy.................$12.50 – 15.00

2nd Row:
Ballerina, 3⅝"..................$17.50 – 20.00
Ballerina, green dress.......$20.00 – 25.00
Ballerina, 4¼" and Ballerina,
    3½"..............................$20.00 – 25.00

3rd Row:
1st, Dancer, blue dress, 4"...$9.00 – 10.00
2nd, Dancer, yellow dress, 3½"..$6.00 – 8.00
3rd and 5th, Dancers, 2½"....$3.00 – 4.00 ea.
4th, Dancer, 3"....................$4.00 – 5.00
6th, Dancer w/Leg Exposed, 4".$6.00 – 8.00

4th Row:
Dancer, orange dress, 3¼"..$9.00 – 10.00
Dancer, 2½"........................$3.00 – 4.00
Dancer................................$3.00 – 4.00
4th – 7th, Dancers.............$3.00 – 4.00 ea.

5th Row:
Ballerina, 5¾"...................$40.00 – 45.00
Wind-swept Lady, 6½".......$20.00 – 25.00
Lady Holding Dress, 6¼"..$20.00 – 25.00
Ballerina w/Turquoise Skirt,
    6¼"..............................$35.00 – 40.00

Page 112

Top Row:
Lady and Gentleman,
    Paired.........................$30.00 – 35.00 ea.

2nd Row:
Dutch Children.................$17.50 – 20.00 ea.
Lady Holding Hat.............$20.00 – 25.00
Dancing Lady...................$25.00 – 30.00

3rd Row:
Tambourine Player...........$20.00 – 25.00

Dancer.............................$25.00 – 30.00
Tiered Skirted Lady..........$25.00 – 30.00

Page 113

Top Row:
Lady Holding Hat.............$20.00 – 25.00
Dutch Sailor w/Bag..........$20.00 – 25.00

Middle:
Lady w/Feathered Hat......$25.00 – 30.00
Lady Holding Hat w/Pink
    Trim............................$30.00 – 35.00

Bottom:
M'Lady w/Basket w/Pink
    Trim............................$30.00 – 35.00
Dutch Girl........................$20.00 – 25.00
Windmill Shakers.............$12.50 – 15.00
Windmill Shakers w/Turning
    Blades........................$30.00 – 35.00

Page 114

Top Row:
Figures 1, 3, 5, and 6..........$8.00 – 10.00
Bisque Figures 2 and 8, Reclining
    Figure........................$10.00 – 12.00
Girl #7...............................$5.00 – 6.00

2nd Row:
Figures 1 and 4.................$8.00 – 10.00
Rickshaw..........................$22.50 – 25.00
Man w/Clay Pots..............$10.00 – 12.00
Shelf Sitter.......................$15.00 – 17.50

3rd Row:
Shelf Sitter.......................$15.00 – 17.50
Figures 2, 3, 4, 5, and 9......$8.00 – 10.00
Figure #6..........................$5.00 – 6.00
Bisque Girl #7...................$12.50 – 15.00

4th Row:
Girls 1 and 7, fine detail....$20.00 – 22.50
Figures 2, 5, and 6............$15.00 – 20.00
3rd Figure........................$20.00 – 25.00
Tall Figure #4, 11"...........$50.00 – 60.00

Page 115

Top Row:
1st, Lady w/Fan, 5"..........$10.00 – 12.50
2nd and 8th, Seated or Standing
    Girls...........................$8.00 – 10.00 ea.
3rd, Dancer, 6¾".............$20.00 – 22.50
4th, Black P. J..................$12.50 – 15.00
5th, Fan Lady...................$20.00 – 25.00
6th, Lady w/Goose...........$15.00 – 17.50
7th, Little Guy..................$8.00 – 10.00

2nd Row:
1st and 2nd, Girl w/Fan and Boy w/Blue
    Top, 4".......................$6.00 – 8.00 ea.
3rd, Smaller version of 2nd....$4.00 – 5.00
4th, 5th, & 8th, Girl w/Fan, Man w/Flute,
    Boy w/Pig....................$12.50 – 15.00 ea.
6th, Guy(?).......................$8.00 – 10.00
7th, Folded Hands, 5⅞"....$12.50 – 15.00

3rd Row:
1st, Lady w/Fan, 7½".......$12.50 – 15.00

2nd and 3rd, Ladies
    w/Fan.........................$12.50 – 15.00 ea.
4th, Gray Lady w/Fan, 8".$15.00 – 17.50
5th and 6th, Couple, 8¼".$40.00 – 50.00 pr.
7th, Dancer, 8".................$22.50 – 25.00
8th, Mandolin Player........$12.50 – 15.00

4th Row:
1st and 2nd, Figurines, 7"..$12.50 – 15.00 ea.
3rd, Lady w/Basket on
    Head, 7⅞"...................$20.00 – 25.00
4th, Man w/Hands in
    Sleeves.......................$20.00 – 22.50
5th and 6th, Matching bases and
    marks..........................$17.50 – 20.00 ea.
7th, Similar to 1st and 2nd..$12.50 – 15.00
8th, Warrior.......................$12.50 – 15.00

Page 116

Top Row:
Girl, 12" tall.....................$40.00 – 45.00
2nd, 4th and 5th Dancers..$20.00 – 25.00 ea.
3rd Dancer......................$17.50 – 20.00 ea.

2nd Row:
1st and 6th Small Figures....$8.00 – 10.00 ea.
2nd and 5th Men, nice detail..$20.00 – 25.00 ea.
3rd Girl with Fan...............$10.00 – 12.50
4th Male Musician.............$8.00 – 10.00

3rd Row:
1st and 5th Small Figures......$6.00 – 7.00 ea.
2nd Performer, Mate to 1st Figure 2nd
    Row............................$8.00 – 10.00
Reclining Man...................$12.50 – 15.00
Couple..............................$8.00 – 10.00

Page 117

Top Row:
Oriental Pair.....................$50.00 – 65.00
Trousered Oriental Pair....$50.00 – 65.00

2nd Row:
First Oriental Pair............$45.00 – 55.00
Black Based Orientals......$40.00 – 50.00

3rd Row:
Coolie Hatted Pair...........$25.00 – 27.50
Animated Pair Orientals...$30.00 – 35.00

4th Row:
Flared Trousered Pair......$35.00 – 40.00
Second Pair......................$35.00 – 40.00

Page 118

Top Row:
Pink Hatted Girl w/Baskets,
    5⅛"..............................$15.00 – 17.50
Similar to 1st, 6"..............$17.50 – 20.00
3rd and 4th, Boys Holding
    Hats............................$15.00 – 17.50 ea.

2nd Row:
1st and 2nd, Couple w/Boy Playing a
    Mandolin.....................$25.00 – 30.00 pr.
3rd and 4th, Wall Plaques.$35.00 – 45.00 pr.

5th and 7th, Violin and Tambourine
  Players ....$8.00 – 10.00 ea.
6th, Mandolin Player ....$8.00 – 10.00

3rd Row:
All ....$8.00 – 10.00 ea.

4th Row:
1st, Fan Girl, 4⅝" ....$8.00 – 10.00
2nd – 6th, All bisque ranging from 4"
  to 4⅝" ....$10.00 – 12.50 ea.

5th Row:
1st, Same as 1st in row above except
  4⅛" ....$6.00 – 8.00
2nd – 9th, All 4⅛" ....$6.00 – 8.00 ea.

Page 119
Top Row:
Couple, 4" ....$10.00 – 12.50 ea.
Couple, 4⅞" ....$12.50 – 15.00 ea.
Couple, 5⅜" ....$12.50 – 15.00 ea.
Bisque Set, 4⅝" ....$12.50 – 15.00 ea.

2nd Row:
Seated Pair, 2¾" ....$20.00 – 25.00
2nd and 3rd, prs. Old and
  Young....$16.00 – 20.00 pr. /$8.00 – 10.00 ea.
Couple, 3⅛" ....$8.00 – 10.00 ea.
Boy and Girl, 4⅝" ....$18.00 – 22.00 pr.

3rd Row:
Couple, 8¼" ....$40.00 – 50.00 pr.
Dancers, 7½" ....$75.00 – 100.00 pr.
Couple, 7" ....$40.00 – 50.00 pr.

4th Row:
1st – 5th, Set, 7½" ....$17.50 – 20.00 ea.
6th – 8th, Set....................$15.00 – 17.50 ea.

Page 120
Top Row:
1st and 3rd, Couple, 6½" ..$25.00 – 30.00 pr.
2nd, Couple, 4"...................$10.00 – 12.00 pr.
4th, Couple w/Pig and
  Duck..........................$25.00 – 30.00 pr.
5th, Couple, 4" ....$15.00 – 20.00 pr.

2nd Row:
1st, Kissing Couple............$30.00 – 32.50
2nd and 3rd same as 1st only marked in
  red..............................$30.00 – 32.50 pr.

3rd Row:
1st and 2nd, Couples, 8¼" ..$60.00 – 75.00 pr.
3rd, Skinny Yellow Couple,
  7¼" ....$25.00 – 30.00 pr.

4th Row:
Similar to Page 119, Row 3 .$40.00 – 50.00 pr.
Older Couple ....$35.00 – 40.00 pr.
Children, 7½" ....$50.00 – 60.00 pr.
Couple, 6⅛" ....$30.00 – 35.00 pr.

Page 121
Top Row:
Grandfather, 6" ....$22.50 – 25.00

Warrior, 8" ....$30.00 – 35.00
Girl w/Bird, 6" ....$20.00 – 22.50
Girl, 7⅛" ....$20.00 – 25.00
5th and 7th, Coolie and Musician, 7" and
  6½"..........................$20.00 – 22.50 ea.
6th, Holding Flowers, 6" ....$18.00 – 20.00

2nd Row:
Lady w/Flowers, 5½"........$18.00 – 20.00
Bended Knee Flower Offering,
  5"................................$15.00 – 18.00
3rd and 5th, Musician and Lady,
  5".........................$12.50 – 15.00 ea.
Girl w/Bow, 4½" ....$10.00 – 12.50

3rd Row:
Instrument Player, 9" ....$40.00 – 45.00
Lady w/Muff, 8" ....$30.00 – 32.50
Musician, 10" ....$60.00 – 65.00
Warrior, 8¼" ....$35.00 – 37.50
Robed Man, 8" ....$32.50 – 35.00
Woman, 7½" ....$25.00 – 27.50

4th Row:
Lady w/Fan, 5", Baldy, 4" ..$8.00 – 10.00 ea.
Coolie, 3¼" ....$6.00 – 8.00
Coolie, 4" ....$8.00 – 10.00
Man w/Rabbits, 4" ....$30.00 – 35.00
Lady w/Fan, 3¾" ....$20.00 – 22.50
Dancer, 4½" ....$12.50 – 15.00

Page 122
Top Row:
Dancers, 5" .....$15.00 ea./$30.00 – 35.00 pr.
Orientals Robed in Red,
  6⅛" ....$15.00 ea./$30.00 – 35.00 pr.
Pair, 5⅞" and 6"..$15.00 ea./$30.00 – 3500 pr.
Pair, 6½" and 6" ..$17.50 ea./$35.00 – 40.00 pr.

2nd Row:
1st & 2nd pairs, all marked the same,
  4½" ....$10.00 ea./$20.00 – 22.50 pr.
"It was this long,"
  4¼" ....$8.00 ea./$16.00 – 20.00 pr.
Musicians, 4½"..$8.00 ea./$16.00 – 20.00 pr.

3rd Row:
Dancers, 7½" ..$25.00 ea./$50.00 – 60.00 pr.
Dancers, 8⅛" ..$30.00 ea./$60.00 – 65.00 pr.
Couple,
  7¾" and 8" ..$30.00 ea./$60.00 – 65.00 pr.

4th Row
Couple, 7½" and 7⅜",
  "Mariyama" ..$22.00 ea./$45.00 – 50.00 pr.
Dancers, 8¾" ..$42.50 ea./$85.00 – 100.00 pr.
Prayerful Couple, 7⅝",
  "Mariyama" .$17.50 ea./$35.00 – 40.00 pr.

Page 123
Top Row:
Black Fiddler, 5" ....$40.00 – 45.00
Black Fiddler, 6" ....$55.00 – 60.00
Indian Squaw, 4½"...........$10.00 – 12.50
Indian (Asian), 6" ....$12.50 – 15.00
Balloon Lady, 5½" ....$45.00 – 50.00

Indian w/Papoose, 5½" ....$20.00 – 22.50
Indian Planter, 3" ....$8.00 – 10.00
Indian Chief, 5½" ....$22.50 – 25.00
Indian Squaw, 6"............$30.00 – 35.00

2nd Row:
Black Band Members, 2¾" ..$20.00 – 22.50 ea.
Chinese Couple, 5¼" ....$20.00 – 22.50
Buddha, 5½" ....$20.00 – 22.50
Incense Burner, 4"...........$20.00 – 22.50
Dancer, 5" ....$22.50 – 25.00
Black Shoeshine Boy, 5½" ..$50.00 – 55.00

3rd Row:
Buddha Gods, 4" to
  4¾" ....$8.00 ea./$56.00 – 65.00 set

4th Row:
Dutch Water Girl, 4" ....$10.00 – 12.50
Dutch Planter, 3", "Pico" ..$12.50 – 15.00
3rd and 5th Delft Ladies,
  6¼"..................$32.50 – 35.00 ea.
Dutch Girl w/Milk Can, 6".$20.00 – 22.50
Dutch Children, 3" ....$10.00 – 12.50 ea.
Dutch Egg Timer w/Sand Timer,
  3½" complete ....$20.00 – 22.50

5th Row:
Eskimos, 3" and 2¾" ....$12.50 – 15.00 ea.
Indian Water Boy, 4" ....$10.00 – 12.00
Indian, 3"............................$8.00 – 10.00
Spanish Guitar Player, 4¼" ..$8.00 – 10.00
Mexican, 5¼" ....$17.50 – 20.00
Martian (?), 3" ....$20.00 – 25.00
Indian Canoe w/Plastic
  Flowers.........................$18.00 – 20.00

Page 124
Top Row:
1st and 2nd, Aborigine Pair,
  4¾"..............................$40.00 – 50.00
Snake Charmer Couple Vase,
  5½" ....$20.00 – 22.50
Black Fiddling Boy ....$20.00 – 22.50
Indian Winding Turban, 6" .$17.50 – 20.00
"Mammy" Pie Bird........$125.00 – 150.00

2nd Row:
Boy w/Fiddle, 3" ....$15.00 – 17.50
Boy w/Horn, 3" ....$15.00 – 17.50
Gray Faced Fiddler ....$12.50 – 15.00
Cowboy on Horse.............$10.00 – 12.50
Cowboy Vase ....$10.00 – 12.50
Indian Girl Bud Vase, 3⅝" ..$8.00 – 10.00
Indian Chief Bud Vase, 3⅝" ..$8.00 – 10.00

3rd Row:
1st and 2nd, Dutch Pair ...$17.50 – 20.00 ea.
Hula Girl w/Grass Skirt......$7.50 – 10.00
Hula Girl ....$10.00 – 12.50
Indian Head Metal Pencil
  Sharpener ....$15.00 – 20.00
Ash Tray, metal, "Howdy
  Podner" ....$4.00 – 5.00
Indian Head ....$12.50 – 15.00

Price Guide →

4th Row:
Dutch Girl, 3¼" ....$5.00 – 6.00
Dutch Girl Shaker ....$6.00 – 8.00
Dutch Boy Bust Shaker ....$6.00 – 8.00
Dutch Boy w/Pipe...............$5.00 – 6.00
Dutch Girl w/Basket, 4½" .$12.50 – 15.00
Dutch Girl w/Basket, 3⅛" ..$6.00 – 8.00
Dutch Girl Seated Shaker.....$6.00 – 8.00
Dutch Boy w/Buckets ....$10.00 – 12.00

5th Row:
Girl with Bowl on Head 4½"..$6.00 – 8.00
Girl w/Bowl on Head and Vase,
 5" ....$8.00 – 10.00
Cowboy, 5⅛" ....$10.00 – 12.00
4th and 5th, Dutch Couple,
 6⅛" ....$17.50 – 20.00 ea.
6th and 7th, Snake
 Charming.....................$30.00 – 35.00 pr.

Page 125
Top Row:
Indian Planter, 7⅛" ....$20.00 – 25.00
American Indian Ash Tray .$10.00 – 12.50
Black Drummer, 5" ....$40.00 – 45.00
Black Horn Player, 6¼" ....$40.00 – 45.00
Cowboy Ash Tray................$3.00 – 4.00
Mexican on Donkey, 8¼" .$25.00 – 30.00

2nd Row:
1st – 5th, Black Musicians, 2¾" .$20.00 – 22.50 ea.
6th and 7th, Dutch Girl and
 Boy ....$12.50 – 15.00 pr.
8th and 9th, Single Dutch
 Shakers.............................$6.00 – 8.00 ea.

3rd Row:
1st and 2nd, Dutch Girl and
 Boy ....$20.00 – 25.00 pr.
Dutch Girl Bell ....$15.00 – 18.00
Seated Dutch Girl ....$12.50 – 15.00
Seated Dutch Boy............$12.50 – 15.00
Small Dutch Girl.................$4.00 – 5.00
Dutch Boy ....$5.00 – 6.00
Single Dutch Shaker ....$6.00 – 8.00

4th Row:
American Indian Lady, 4¼" ..$6.00 – 8.00
American Indian in Canoe .$10.00 – 12.50
Cowgirl on Horse ....$6.00 – 8.00
Cowboy or Mexican Drummer.$5.00 – 6.00
Cowgirl............................$8.00 – 10.00
Mexican Guitar Player.........$5.00 – 6.00
Cowboy ....$8.00 – 10.00

5th Row:
1st and 2nd, Indian Couple,
 6⅛"..............................$30.00 – 35.00 pr.
3rd, Organ Grinder..........$20.00 – 22.50
4th American Indian Chief, 5⅟₁₆".$15.00 – 20.00
5th, Hawaiian Girl w/Guitar.$10.00 – 12.50
6th and 7th, Hula Girls ....$8.00 – 10.00 ea.

Page 126
Top Row:
Musical Couples..............$40.00 – 50.00 pr.

2nd Row:
First Pair (Bisque), Approx. 10" ..$85.00 – 100.00
Second Pair ....$25.00 – 30.00
Pair Dancers (Bisque), 10" .$60.00 – 70.00

3rd Row:
1st and 3rd Pair, Seated...$60.00 – 75.00
2nd Pair, Orientals Bisque, Approx.
 9"...............................$60.00 – 75.00

Page 127
Top Row:
1st Pair ....$4.00 – 5.00
Pairs 2 and 5 ....$12.00 – 14.00
3rd Pair ....$16.00 – 20.00
4th Pair ....$30.00 – 35.00
6th Pair ....$10.00 – 12.00

2nd Row:
Pairs 1 and 5 ....$25.00 – 30.00
Pairs 2 and 3 ....$18.00 – 22.00
4th Pair ....$12.50 – 15.00

3rd Row:
1st Figure........................$12.00 – 15.00
2nd Figure.......................$12.00 – 15.00
Figures 3 and 4 ....$35.00 – 40.00 pr.
Figures 5 and 6 ....$12.50 – 15.00 pr.

4th Row:
Pairs 1 and 3, nice detail ..$70.00 – 80.00 pr.
2nd Pair, Signed Andrea.$100.00 – 125.00 pr.

Page 128
Top Row:
Hatted Colonials, Approx.
 12" pr ....$75.00 – 90.00
Red-Haired Colonials,
 11½" pr ....$60.00 – 75.00

2nd Row:
First and Third Pair, Approx.
 10".............................$60.00 – 75.00
Second Pair Colonials,
 11½"pr ....$80.00 – 85.00

3rd Row:
First and Fourth Pairs, Approx.
 6" pr ....$30.00 – 35.00
Musical Pair.....................$45.00 – 50.00
Pair in Blue Tones............$30.00 – 35.00

Page 129
Top Row:
Colonial Couple ....$125.00 – 150.00 pr.

2nd Row:
Couple in Blue and Pink, 12" ..$100.00 – 115.00

3rd Row:
Hatted Pair, Approx. 12".$100.00 – 120.00
Courting Couple, Approx.
 12"..............................$75.00 – 90.00

Bottom Row:
Musicians Couple, Approx.
 10"..............................$75.00 – 85.00

Seated pair, 6" ....$40.00 – 50.00

Page 130
Top Row:
Couple, 7¼" ....$40.00 – 55.00
Couple, 6½" ....$100.00 – 125.00
Couple, 7½" ....$50.00 – 55.00

2nd Row:
Couple, 5" ....$25.00 – 30.00
Couple w/Dogs, 5½" ....$30.00 – 40.00
Couple w/Arms Up and
 Dogs.........................$45.00 – 55.00
Dutch People at Well........$30.00 – 35.00

3rd Row:
Colonial Couple, 10⅛"....$90.00 – 110.00
Couple, 10" ....$75.00 – 90.00

4th Row:
Couple w/Hats, 6½" ....$50.00 – 60.00
Couple Courting ....$75.00 – 100.00
Couple, 6½" ....$40.00 – 50.00

Page 131
Top Row:
Couple, 6⅛" ....$30.00 – 40.00
Couple, 6" ....$50.00 – 60.00
Couple, 7" ....$30.00 – 35.00
Couple, 5¼" ....$30.00 – 35.00

2nd Row:
Couple, 5¼" ....$45.00 – 55.00
Couple, 4⅝" ....$20.00 – 25.00
Couple.............................$20.00 – 25.00
Dutch Couple, 4⅛" ....$20.00 – 25.00
Colonial Couple ....$15.00 – 20.00
Couple in White ....$15.00 – 20.00

3rd Row:
Couple, 7½" ....$50.00 – 60.00
Colonial Couple, 7¼"........$60.00 – 70.00
Couple, 8⅛" ....$80.00 – 90.00
Couple, 7" ....$40.00 – 50.00

4th Row:
Couple, 6⅛" ....$35.00 – 40.00
Hatted Couple ....$25.00 – 30.00
Musical Couple ....$40.00 – 50.00
Couple, 6⅜" ....$35.00 – 40.00

Page 132
Top Row:
Double Pair,
 6" ....$35.00 ea./$70.00 – 80.00 pr.
Courting Couple Double,
 6" ....$60.00 ea./$120.00 – 130.00 pr.

2nd Row:
Busts, 5½" ......$20.00 ea./$40.00 – 50.00 pr.
Trio, 4" and 3¾" ....$12.50 – 15.00 ea.
Seated Couple,
 5½" ....$40.00 ea./$80.00 – 90.00 pr.

3rd Row:
Double, 4¾" ....$12.50 ea./$25.00 – 30.00 pr.

Musician and Friend,
   5" ....$15.00 ea./$30.00 – 35.00 pr.
Couple, 5" ......$10.00 ea./$ 20.00 – 25.00 pr.

4th Row:
Flower Holders,
   7" ....$35.00 ea./$70.00 – 80.00 pr.
Shepherds,
   13½" ....$85.00 ea./$170.00 – 195.00 pr.
Dancers, 6¼" and
   6" ....$20.00 ea./$40.00 – 45.00 pr.
White Dancers,
   6¼" ....$15.00 ea./$30.00 – 35.00 pr.

Page 133

Top Row:
Colonial Couple, 5⅝" ....$30.00 – 35.00
Colonial Couple, 8¹/₁₆".......$70.00 – 80.00
Couple, 7" ....$50.00 – 60.00

2nd Row:
Couple, 4⅛" ....$20.00 – 25.00
2nd Couple w/Flowers ......$25.00 – 30.00
3rd Couple in Fancy Dress..$15.00 – 20.00
4th Blue Couple................$25.00 – 30.00

3rd Row:
1st and 2nd Couples, 5" ....$25.00 – 30.00 pr.
3rd Couple ....$20.00 – 25.00
4th Colonial Couple ....$30.00 – 35.00

4th Row:
Pastel Couple, 5" ....$25.00 – 30.00
Couple...............................$20.00 – 25.00
Couple...............................$20.00 – 25.00
Couple, 4" ....$18.00 – 20.00

5th Row:
Musical Couple, 4⅝" ....$25.00 – 30.00
2nd Seated Musicians, 4⅛"$25.00 – 30.00
3rd Same as 2nd, 3½" ......$15.00 – 20.00
4th Seated, 3" pr. ....$30.00 – 35.00

Page 134

Top Row:
1st and 2nd, Pair, 6¼" ......$45.00 – 60.00
3rd and 4th, Pair, 7½".......$40.00 – 50.00
5th and 6th, Colonial Pair,
   8"...................................$55.00 – 65.00

2nd Row:
1st and 2nd, Pair Dancers,
   5¼"..................................$30.00 – 35.00
3rd and 4th, Pair w/Baskets,
   5½"..................................$35.00 – 40.00
5th and 6th, Dutch Pair, 4⅛"..$20.00 – 25.00
7th and 8th, Colonial Pair, 5½"..$30.00 – 35.00

3rd Row:
1st and 2nd, Pair Musicians,
   10⅛"...............................$110.00 – 125.00
3rd and 4th, Pair in Yellow,
   10"...................................$125.00 – 150.00
5th and 6th, Pair Dutch Peasants,
   8¼"..................................$55.00 – 65.00

4th Row:
1st and 2nd, Colonial Pair,
   6⅛"..................................$40.00 – 50.00
3rd and 4th, Colonial Pair,
   6½"..................................$50.00 – 60.00
5th and 6th, Dutch Pair.....$17.50 – 20.00
7th and 8th, Fancy Laced
   Pair ....$40.00 – 50.00

Page 135

Top Row:
Couple at Piano, 4" ....$30.00 – 35.00
Dancing Couple, 4½" ....$20.00 – 25.00
Triple, 3" ....$12.50 – 15.00
Romantic Couple, 4"..........$25.00 – 30.00
Couple, 4½", "Canadian National Exhibition,
   Toronto, Canada" ....$20.00 – 25.00
Couple, 4" ....$15.00 – 18.00

2nd Row:
1st and 4th Serenading Couple,
   5¼" and 5⅛".................$20.00 – 22.50 ea.
Coach, et al, 5¾" x 7" ....$75.00 – 85.00
Serenading Couple, 4½" ..$20.00 – 22.50
Triple w/Piano, 3¾" ....$30.00 – 35.00

3rd Row:
Couple Waiting for Rain, 5½",
   "Highmount" ....$25.00 – 30.00
2nd and 3rd Couples, 5½" and
   5¼"..................................$20.00 – 25.00 ea.
4th, 5th, and 6th Couples, 4¼" to
   3¾"..................................$15.00 – 18.00 ea.
Couple, 4½" ....$17.50 – 20.00

4th Row:
1st, 3rd, and 4th Couples, 6⅞" to
   6⅜"..................................$40.00 – 50.00 ea.
Musicians, 7" x 7⅞", Villain and Captive,
   7½"..................................$65.00 – 75.00 ea.

Page 136

Top Row:
1st and 3rd, Sled Couple,
   5¾"..................................$200.00 – 225.00 pr.
2nd, Courting Couple, 6¼"..$60.00 – 70.00

2nd Row:
1st and 4th, Couples, 5½" .$20.00 – 25.00 ea.
2nd and 3rd, Couples........$25.00 – 30.00 ea.

3rd Row:
1st and 3rd, Couples, 4" ....$20.00 – 25.00 ea.
2nd, Couple......................$12.50 – 15.00
4th, Couple, 5"...................$25.00 – 30.00
5th, Couple.......................$25.00 – 30.00

4th Row:
Man in Hat, 3¾"...............$17.50 – 20.00
Triple Figure ....$20.00 – 25.00
Seated Couple w/Dog.......$40.00 – 45.00
Musician Lady and Fellow..$25.00 – 30.00
Couple at Piano................$15.00 – 18.00
Couple..............................$15.00 – 18.00

5th Row:
Cellist Lady and Fellow, 3½" ..$25.00 – 30.00
Couple w/Dog ....$15.00 – 18.00
Couples, 2⅜"....................$4.00 – 5.00
Dancers.............................$6.00 – 8.00
Couples, 2⅜"....................$5.00 – 6.00
Couple................................$6.00 – 8.00
Skirt Lifter.........................$15.00 – 18.00

Page 137

Top Row:
Colonial Couple in Blue, 4¾"..$15.00 – 18.00
Couple w/Man in Yellow
   Cape ....$20.00 – 25.00
Couple w/Hats ....$15.00 – 18.00
Man Whispering in Her Ear .$25.00 – 30.00
Fence Sitters.....................$15.00 – 20.00
Mandolin Wooing..............$12.50 – 15.00

2nd Row:
1st, Seated Couple w/Book,
   3⅜"..................................$12.50 – 15.00
2nd, 4th, and 7th, Couples.$12.50 – 15.00 ea.
3rd, 5th, and 8th Couples ..$12.50 – 15.00 ea.
6th, Removing or Putting on
   Coat ....$15.00 – 18.00

3rd Row:
Dancing Couple, 7¼" ....$35.00 – 40.00
Cinderella and Prince
   Charming.........................$150.00 – 175.00
Couple, 7⅛" ....$40.00 – 45.00
Dancers, 6⅛" ....$30.00 – 35.00

4th Row:
1st, Colonial Seated, 3⅝"..$10.00 – 12.50
2nd, 5th, and 7th, Couples.$12.50 – 15.00 ea.
3rd and 4th, Couples, 5½".$20.00 – 25.00 ea.
6th, Wooden Looking Couple .$15.00 – 17.50

Page 138

Top Row:
Couple at Piano, 5½" ....$75.00 – 85.00
Lady w/Fan and Man w/Hat,
   6⅜"..................................$50.00 – 60.00
Man Wooing Lady w/Flute,
   6⅞"..................................$75.00 – 90.00

2nd Row:
Couple w/Lady Playing Mandolin,
   5½"..................................$50.00 – 60.00
Couple w/Man Playing
   Mandolin ....$25.00 – 30.00
Seated Couple ....$12.50 – 15.00
Couple..............................$20.00 – 25.00

3rd Row:
1st and 2nd, Colonial Pair,
   4⅛"..................................$30.00 – 35.00 pr.
3rd and 4th, Couple Pair...$35.00 – 40.00 pr.
5th and 6th, Mandolin-Playing Man
   Pair, 4⅜" ....$40.00 – 45.00 pr.

4th Row:
1st and 2nd, Couple, 5"....$40.00 – 50.00 pr.
3rd and 4th, Couple, 3¾" ..$20.00 – 25.00 pr.

Price Guide —

5th and 6th, Slightly different
    sizes ....$30.00 – 35.00 ea.

5th Row:
1st, Dancing Couple, 3⅛"..$10.00 – 12.00
2nd – 5th, Couples, 2¼" to 2½"..$5.00 – 6.00 ea.
6th, Couple......................$12.50 – 15.00
7th, Couple Seated...........$12.50 – 15.00

Page 139
Top Row:
1st, Man w/Blue Coat, 6"..$20.00 – 22.50
2nd, 4th, and 5th, Men......$20.00 – 22.50 ea.
3rd, Man w/Emblem in Red.$22.50 – 25.00
6th, Mandolin Player.........$25.00 – 30.00
7th and 8th, Men.............$12.50 – 15.00 ea.

2nd Row:
1st, Balloon Man, 3½".......$15.00 – 18.00
2nd and 3rd, Men ....$8.00 – 10.00 ea.
4th – 8th, Men ....$6.00 – 8.00 ea.
9th and 10th, Men ....$8.00 – 10.00 ea.

3rd Row:
1st – 3rd, Men, 4⅛" ....$6.00 – 8.00 ea.
4th – 6th Men ....$4.00 – 5.00 ea.
7th and 8th, Men ....$8.00 – 10.00 ea.
9th and 10th, Men ....$10.00 – 12.00 ea.
11th, Man Holding Flower.$12.50 – 15.00

4th Row:
1st, Man w/Violin, 8⅛" ......$40.00 – 50.00
2nd, Man w/Tricorn Hat, 9⅝" .$50.00 – 60.00
3rd and 4th, Mandolin Players,
    10⅛".........................$60.00 – 75.00 ea.
5th, Man w/Blue Coat and Tricorn Hat,
    10⅝".......................$85.00 – 100.00
6th, Swashbuckler, 10".......$60.00 – 75.00

Page 140
Top Row:
Man with Hat, 7¼" ....$27.50 – 30.00
2nd and 3rd Men, 8" ....$35.00 – 40.00 ea.
Man, 7½".......................$27.50 – 30.00
Seated, 6¼" ....$25.00 – 30.00

2nd Row:
Man with Flowers, 5" ....$15.00 – 17.50
2nd, 5th, and 6th Men, 4"..$12.50 – 15.00 ea.
3rd Man, 3"......................$8.00 – 10.00
4th Man, 3½" ....$8.00 – 10.00
7th Waver, 5½" ....$20.00 – 22.50

3rd Row:
1st and 2nd Men, 6" and 6½".$30.00 – 35.00 ea.
Bottle Boy, 5¼"...............$18.00 – 20.00
4th and 5th Men, 6½" and 6"..$20.00 – 22.50 ea.
Violinist, 5⅜" ....$12.50 – 15.00

4th Row:
1st and 5th Men, 8" and 7½"..$35.00 – 40.00 ea.
Uniformed Man, 10⅜" ....$60.00 – 65.00
Colonial, 10"...................$65.00 – 75.00
Red Head, 9¾" ....$65.00 – 75.00

Page 141
Top Row:
Blue Boy, 7⅝" ....$35.00 – 40.00
Man in Striped Pants........$25.00 – 30.00
Peasant...........................$15.00 – 20.00
Man Scratching Head........$17.50 – 20.00
Man in Pink Pants............$20.00 – 25.00
Man in Plaid Shirt and Blue
    Pants.........................$20.00 – 25.00
Colonial Man....................$20.00 – 25.00
Man w/Hand to Lips ....$12.00 – 15.00

2nd Row:
1st, Sharp Dresser, 5".......$10.00 – 12.50
2nd, White w/Brownish Finish..$10.00 – 12.50
3rd, 7th, 8th, and 10th, Men..$6.00 – 8.00 ea.
4th, Colonial Man ....$6.00 – 8.00
5th and 6th, Men ....$12.50 – 15.00 ea.
9th, Colonial ....$6.00 – 8.00

3rd Row:
1st, Flute Player, 5"............$8.00 – 10.00
2nd, 7th, and 8th, Men ....$8.00 – 10.00 ea.
3rd, 4th, and 6th, Men.........$8.00 – 10.00 ea.
5th, Man in Yellow Coat ......$5.00 – 6.00
9th, Seated Man ....$5.00 – 6.00
10th, Man in White w/Brown..$10.00 – 12.00

4th Row:
1st and 5th, Colonial Men, 4".$8.00 – 10.00 ea.
2nd and 3rd, Musketeer and
    Colonial ....$6.00 – 8.00 ea.
4th, 7th, and 8th, Colonial
    Men................................$3.00 – 4.00 ea.
6th, Man w/Hat Under Arm..$6.00 – 8.00
9th, Fiddler.....................$10.00 – 12.00
10th, Guitar Player ....$10.00 – 12.00

5th Row:
1st, Man Bowing, 6"..........$20.00 – 22.50
2nd, Man w/Basket...........$12.50 – 15.00
3rd and 7th, Colonial Men.$15.00 – 17.50 ea.
4th and 6th, Musicians ......$17.50 – 20.00 ea.
5th, Cowboy ....$17.50 – 20.00
8th, Man w/Yellow Cape...$15.00 – 17.50

Page 142
Top Row:
1st, 2nd, and 3rd Ladies, 4" .$8.00 – 10.00 ea.
4th, 5th, and 6th Dancers, 3¾" and
    4".............................$10.00 – 12.50 ea.
Ballerina, 4½" ....$22.50 – 25.00
Ballerina, 5¾" ....$35.00 – 40.00

2nd Row:
1st, 3rd, and 4th Figures, 5¼" and
    5"..............................$18.00 – 20.00 ea.
2nd Cellist, 3¼" ....$12.50 – 15.00
5th and 7th Figurines, 4¼" ..$12.50 – 15.00
6th Figure, 4" ....$10.00 – 12.00

3rd Row:
Lady, 5" ....$15.00 – 18.00
2nd, 6th, and 8th Ladies, 4¾" and
    5"..............................$10.00 – 12.50 ea.

3rd and 5th Flower Ladies, 5" and
    5¾"............................$12.50 – 15.00 ea.
4th and 7th Ladies, 4" and
    4¼"............................$10.00 – 12.50 ea.

4th Row:
1st and 11th Figurines, 7"and
    6¼"............................$20.00 – 22.50 ea.
2nd, 4th, and 8th Flower Ladies, 4¼"
    and 4"........................$10.00 – 12.50 ea.
3rd Mandolin Player, 10¼".$50.00 – 60.00
5th Lady, 12¼" ....$75.00 – 90.00
6th Windy Flower Girl, 5".$15.00 – 17.50
7th and 9th Ladies, 7" and
    6¾"............................$27.50 – 30.00 ea.
10th Peddler, 3½" ....$8.00 – 10.00

Page 143
Top Row:
1st, Lady w/Basket, 5¾" ....$8.00 – 10.00
2nd and 6th, Lady w/Fan or
    Basket.........................$10.00 – 12.50 ea.
3rd, Lady w/Purple Skirt..$15.00 – 18.00
4th, Brown/White Lady, 8¼" .$30.00 – 40.00
5th, Lady Lifting Skirt ....$20.00 – 22.00
7th, Peasant Lady...........$15.00 – 17.50

2nd Row:
1st, Lady w/Mandolin, 4" ......$6.00 – 8.00
2nd, 4th, and 5th, Ladies...$12.00 – 14.00 ea.
3rd, Gent, 3¾" ....$4.00 – 5.00
6th, 8th, and 9th, Ladies........$5.00 – 6.00 ea.
7th, Lady w/Basket, 5⅜" ..$12.50 – 15.00
10th, Lady, K.J. in emblem ...$5.00 – 6.00

3rd Row:
1st, Lady w/Red Shawl, 3½"..$5.00 – 6.00
2nd – 4th, Ladies w/Dog or Deer,
    4½"............................$17.50 – 20.00 ea.
5th and 8th, Ladies, 5" ......$15.00 – 17.50 ea.
6th and 7th, Ladies ....$6.00 – 8.00 ea.

4th Row:
1st and 6th, Ladies, 7⅛"..$25.00 – 30.00 ea.
2nd, Well Endowed Lady, 8".$30.00 – 35.00
3rd, Lady w/Feathers in Hair,
    10⅜"..........................$75.00 – 90.00
4th, Buxom Lady, 10" ....$75.00 – 90.00
5th, Peasant Lady, 8" ....$30.00 – 35.00

Page 144
Top Row:
1st and 5th Orientals.........$17.50 – 20.00 ea.
2nd and 4th Orientals........$25.00 – 30.00 ea.
3rd (seen as lamp base).....$25.00 – 30.00

2nd Row:
1st Colonial ....$25.00 – 30.00
Lady with Dog..................$25.00 – 30.00
Lady with Net Dress.........$50.00 – 60.00
Gaucho with Guitar ....$17.50 – 20.00
Lady in Pink and White.....$12.00 – 14.00

3rd Row:
Colonial in Tri-Cornered Hat,
    10"..............................$30.00 – 35.00

Lady with Horn, Approx. 10" .$30.00 – 35.00
Lady with Accordion, Approx.
   10"............................$30.00 – 35.00

Page 145
Top Row:
Lady w/Tambourine, 4¾" ....$8.00 – 10.00
Lady in White and Gold ....$10.00 – 12.00
Lady w/Rust Top ....$6.00 – 8.00
Lady w/Feathered Hat, 6"..$12.50 – 15.00
Mexican Lady, 7¼"..........$35.00 – 40.00
Lady Holding Hat.............$12.50 – 15.00
Lady in Yellow and Blue
   Dress......................$15.00 – 18.00
Lady w/Basket ....$10.00 – 12.00

2nd Row:
1st, Lady w/Surprised Expression,
   5"........................$15.00 – 17.50
2nd, Holding Green Dress.$12.50 – 15.00
3rd, Yellow Top w/Bow in Hair.$5.00 – 6.00
4th, Lady w/Rust Top ....$6.00 – 8.00
5th, Lady Holding Hat.......$12.50 – 15.00
6th, 7th, 9th and 10th, Ladies.$10.00 – 12.50 ea.
8th, Lady in Pink and Blue....$3.00 – 4.00

3rd Row:
1st, Lady w/Scottie, 4½"...$15.00 – 18.00
2nd and 7th, Lady in White and Seated
   Lady......................$12.50 – 15.00 ea.
3rd and 4th, Ladies in Yellow Floral
   Skirts....................$15.00 – 17.50 ea.
5th, Lady Reading Book, 5".$22.50 – 25.00
6th, Crinoline Dress Lady,
   5⅝"......................$40.00 – 45.00

4th Row:
Lady w/Crown and Scepter, 8⅛".$40.00 – 45.00
Lady Reading Book, 8⅜"..$35.00 – 40.00
Buxom Lady Holding Fan
   9¾"......................$50.00 – 55.00
Dutch Lady w/Flowers,
   10⅛".....................$40.00 – 50.00
Girl w/Apron, 8¼"...........$30.00 – 35.00
Well Endowed Dancer ......$20.00 – 25.00

Page 146
Top Row:
1st to 4th Stemware, 4¼" to 5¼"w/
   Label....................$15.00 – 17.50 ea.
   w/o Label ....$2.00 – 3.00 ea.

2nd Row:
Pink Atomizer ....$30.00 – 35.00
Blue Atomizer ....$30.00 – 35.00
Perfume Set (4pc.) ....$45.00 – 50.00 set
Blue Cologne and Atomizer on blue
   tray (3pc).................$50.00 – 55.00 set

3rd Row:
Blue Atomizer ....$30.00 – 35.00
Animals w/Paper Stickers ..$10.00 – 12.50 ea.

4th Row:
Parrot Lamp (working) ......$75.00 – 85.00
   (nonworking) ....$40.00 – 45.00

Crystal Perfume and Stopper.$20.00 – 25.00
Green Atomizers..............$30.0 – 35.000 ea.
   $60.00 – 70.00........................pr.

5th Row:
Perfume, pink or blue.........$30.00 – 35.00 ea.
Blue Perfume ....$30.00 – 35.00 ea.
Perfume, green or blue ......$30.00 – 35.00 ea.
Pink Perfume....................$30.00 – 35.00
Blue Perfume w/Unusual
   Stopper ....$35.00 – 40.00

Page 147
Top Row:
Wind Chimes ....$30.00 – 35.00
   With box add $5.00
2nd Row:
Pink Cologne ....$30.00 – 35.00
Small Animals with Sticker..$10.00 – 12.50 ea.
Perfume Bottles ....$30.00 – 35.00 ea.

3rd Row:
Perfume Bottles ....$30.00 – 35.00 ea.
Salt & Pepper Shakers .....$12.50 – 15.00 pr.
Girl with Egg Timer..........$12.50 – 15.00

4th Row:
Toy Binoculars ....$15.00 – 17.50
Perfume & Atomizer Set ...$60.00 – 70.00
Perfume Bottle ....$30.00 – 35.00
Mustard & Lid..................$15.00 – 17.50

Page 148
Top Row:
1st and 2nd, Elephant Sets ..$25.00 – 35.00 ea.
3rd and 5th, Blue Atomizers..$25.00 – 30.00 ea.
4th, Blue Perfume.............$20.00 – 25.00
6th, Icon, 5⅛".................$30.00 – 40.00

2nd Row:
Left: Stemware..................$12.00 – 15.00 ea.
Small Cordial, 1 oz. ....$15.00 – 20.00
Right: Illustration of paper label on stemware

3rd Row:
Left: Blue Horse...............$12.00 – 15.00
Right: Knight Decanter....$75.00 – 100.00

Page 149
Top Row:
Strand of Pearls,.............$10.00 – 12.50 ea.
   Package of 10...........$100.00 – 125.00
"Butterfly Brooch," Card of
   24.........................$30.00 – 40.00
Strand of Pearls...............$12.50 – 15.00
Strand of Miniature Beads .$15.00 – 17.50

2nd Row:
Rhinestone Bracelet ....$30.00 – 50.00
Rhinestone Bracelet ....$30.00 – 50.00
Crossed Swords Pin ....$12.50 – 15.00
4th – 8th, Celluloid Pins.....$10.00 – 15.00 ea.

3rd Row:
Scottie Dog in Sweater .....$15.00 – 20.00

Dog Head ....$12.50 – 18.00
3rd – 5th, Celluloid Bird
   Pins ....$10.00 – 12.50 ea.

4th Row:
1st, Two Dog Head Pin.....$12.50 – 15.00
2nd-4th, Celluloid Brooch and Earring
   Set ....$30.00 – 35.00
5th, Shamrock ....$2.00 – 3.00
6th, Two Dog Head Pin ....$12.50 – 15.00

Page 150
Top Row:
Tray, Five Part, Handled/Very
   Heavy ....$75.00 – 100.00
Wine Goblet ....$12.00 – 15.00

2nd Row:
Cup and Saucer, Sets........$20.00 – 22.50 ea.
Bowl and Spoon (missing
   underplate) ....$15.00 – 18.00

Page 151
Top Row:
Ice Bucket, 7⅝" ....$50.00 – 60.00
Vase w/Leaf Design, 13"..$125.00 – 150.00
Bowl w/Pagoda Scene .....$30.00 – 40.00

2nd Row:
Black Box, 5½" x 9".........$50.00 – 65.00
Five Leaf Clover Tray ....$40.00 – 50.00
Red Box..........................$50.00 – 65.00

3rd Row:
1st, Candy Tray w/Metal
   Handle.......................$20.00 – 25.00
2nd, Cup w/Rattan Handle.$15.00 – 17.50
3rd, Piano ....$40.00 – 50.00
4th and 5th, Vases............$30.00 – 40.00 ea.
6th, Basket......................$65.00 – 75.00

Page 152
Top Row:
Lady, 6" ....$40.00 – 50.00
Corner Shelf, 9¼" ....$45.00 – 50.00
Chest, 3" x 4¼" ....$50.00 – 60.00

2nd Row:
Coaster, 4¼" ....$3.50 – 4.00 ea.
Box, 5" x 2" w/4 Coasters.$27.50 – 30.00 set
Dancer, 4¼" ....$25.00 – 30.00
Box Set of Coasters.........$27.50 – 30.00 set
Coaster, 4¼" for set ....$3.50 – 4.00 ea.

3rd Row:
Relish, 3-part, 5¾" x 15"...$60.00 – 70.00
Wooden Coaster Box and six 2¾"
   Coasters......................$30.00 – 35.00 set

4th Row:
Salt Box, 5" x 5" ....$60.00 – 75.00
Corner Shelf, 13¾" ....$65.00 – 75.00
Dancer, 4" ....$20.00 – 25.00
Wooden Clothes Hanger, 10" x
   10"..............................$22.50 – 25.00

Price Guide ~

Wooden Salad Bowl, 10" ..$15.00 – 17.50
Wooden Salad Bowl, 6" ....$6.00 – 7.50 ea.

Page 153
Plates ....$4.50 – 5.00
Coasters, 2 Sizes ....$3.50 – 4.00
Wall Shelf Unit ....$50.00 – 65.00
Lamp Base ....$75.00 – 85.00
Jce Bucket and Tongs ......$50.00 – 60.00
Salad Bowl w/Fork and
    Spoon ....$30.00 – 40.00
Bowl w/6 Jndividual Bowls and
    Spoon ....$50.00 – 60.00

Page 154
Clockwise from top left:
Cloverleaf Flower Arranger, Two Part
    (2 views) ....$70.00 – 80.00
Cigar Humidor ....$100.00 – 125.00
Ash Trays ....$20.00 – 25.00 ea.
Oval Celery Tray ....$35.00 – 40.00
Rectangle Two-Handled
    Tray ....$75.00 – 80.00

Page 155
Book...................................$75.00 – 85.00

Page 156
Top Row:
Umbrella, 18" ....$25.00 – 30.00
Umbrella, 22" ....$30.00 – 35.00

2nd Row:
Party Horns, 12¼" ....$6.00 – 8.00
Paper Lantern, 4¼" ....$10.00 – 12.50
Needles, 50 asst. ....$12.50 – 15.00

3rd Row:
Orange Fan, 7¾" spine.....$10.00 – 12.50
Blue Fan, 8¾" ....$15.00 – 17.50
Party Favor........................$8.00 – 10.00

4th Row:
Satin Flower Bunch...........$15.00 – 20.00
Pink and Blue Fan, 8½" ....$15.00 – 17.50
Fan, 13¼" w/ Black Handle ..$25.00 – 30.00
Pink Flower Bunch, 8½" .....$8.00 – 10.00
Flower Fan, 8½" ....$15.00 – 17.50

5th Row:
Pink Poseys, 4¼" ....$7.50 – 8.00
Flag, 1⅞" ....$2.00 – 3.00
Needle Assortment ....$12.50 – 15.00
Party Foldout, 6" ....$5.00 – 6.00
String Bowl, 5¾" ....$20.00 – 25.00

Page 157
Large Umbrella, 22" before
    open ....$30.00 – 35.00 ea.
Open Umbrella..................$20.00 – 25.00
"Transfer Picture" Books,
    intact ....$30.00 – 50.00 ea.
Floral Fans........................$15.00 – 17.50 ea.
Large Black Fan..............$20.00 – 25.00

Small Black Fan ....$12.50 – 15.00

Page 158
Top Row:
Fans ....$15.00 – 17.50 ea.
Coolie Pincushion ....$17.50 – 20.00

2nd Row:
Whetstone.......................$10.00 – 12.00
Boat ....$12.00 – 15.00
Shamrocks w/Label ....$2.00 – 3.00 ea.
Prayer Beads ....$25.00 – 30.00
Sewing Kit.......................$15.00 – 20.00

Bottom Row:
Needle Packets.................$17.50 – 20.00 ea.

Page 159
Top Row:
Trays..................................$6.00 – 8.00 ea.
Jack-O-Lantern................$50.00 – 75.00

2nd Row:
Coaster ....$2.00 – 3.00
Purses ....$40.00 – 50.00 ea.

Page 160
Top Row:
Coaster ....$2.00 – 3.00
Round Serving Plate ....$10.00 – 12.00
Rectangular Tray ....$15.00 – 17.50
Small Rectangular Tray ......$8.00 – 10.00
Box of Eight Coasters.......$30.00 – 35.00

2nd Row:
1st, Box of Eight Coasters $30.00 – 35.00
2nd and 7th, Paper Birds..$15.00 – 20.00 ea.
3rd, Coaster.......................$2.00 – 3.00
4th, Red Round Serving Plate.$10.00 – 12.00
5th, Small Rectangular Tray .$8.00 – 10.00
6th, Souvenir Plate ....$12.50 – 15.00

3rd Row:
Pink Barn........................$20.00 – 22.50
Red Bowl ....$12.50 – 15.00
American Flag ....$2.00 – 3.00 ea.
Small Rectangular Tray ......$8.00 – 10.00
Green Church ....$20.00 – 22.50
Black Round Serving Plate .$10.00 – 12.00
Blue House......................$20.00 – 22.50

Page 161
Top Row:
Wooden Cigarette Box,
    3½" x 5".......................$35.00 – 40.00
Wooden Jewelry Box,
    7½" x 7¾"...................$65.00 – 75.00
Bead String, 60" long........$25.00 – 30.00
Chest, 2 drawer, 3" x 4½" .$20.00 – 25.00

2nd Row:
Crocheted Purse, 5" x 8½" $60.00 – 75.00
Wooden Box, 4" x 7" ....$30.00 – 35.00
Butterfly Brooches ....$1.50 – 2.00 ea.

Bead Purse, 7" x 7½" ....$60.00 – 75.00

3rd Row:
Geisha Dancer Music Box,
    12" x 5" ....$150.00 – 175.00
Rosary Beads, 30"..........$30.00 – 35.00
Pearls, 16" ....$30.00 – 35.00
Harmonica Bracelet, 7½"..$20.00 – 25.00
Pearl Bracelet..................$18.00 – 20.00
Gold Expansion Bracelet ..$20.00 – 25.00
Purple Beads, 24"............$18.00 – 20.00

Page 162
Top Row:
Picnic Basket ....$75.00 – 85.00

2nd Row:
Cigarette Dispenser ....$25.00 – 30.00
Trays..................................$4.00 – 5.00 ea.

3rd Row:
Bamboo Dipper ....$25.00 – 30.00
Salad Bowl ....$6.00 – 8.00
Coaster Box and 6 Coasters .$30.00 – 35.00

Page 163
Left:
Lamp..............................$125.00 – 150.00

Right:
1st, Lamp, 13" ....$35.00 – 40.00
2nd, Lamp, 10"................$40.00 – 45.00
3rd, Glass Lamps,
    12" ....$70.00 ea. or 150.00 – 160.00 pr.

Page 164
Top Row:
Standing Colonial Couple ..$40.00 – 50.00 ea.
    Pair ....$80.00 – 90.00
Seated Colonial Couple.....$45.00 – 50.00 ea.
    Pair ....$90.00 – 100.00

2nd Row:
Oriental Dancer ....$35.00 – 40.00
Colonial Lady...................$25.00 – 30.00
Colonial Couple ....$40.00 – 45.00
Lamp Base with Fish Nodder
    Jnset ....$30.00 – 35.00

Page 165
Top Row:
Bisque Lamps ....$60.00 – 75.00 ea.
    Pair ....$120.00 – 150.00
3rd Lamp ....$50.00 – 60.00

2nd Row:
Mary and Lamb ....$75.00 – 100.00
"Wedgwood" Types ....$45.00 – 50.00 ea.

Page 166
Top Row:
1st and 3rd, Colonial Pair .$75.00 – 90.00
2nd, Lamp, 8⅜"................$35.00 – 40.00

2nd Row:
1st and 2nd, Colonial Couple,
  7⅛".................................$80.00 – 90.00 pr.
3rd, Colonial Couple,
  7⅝" x 5⅛"....................$35.00 – 40.00
4th, Lamp, same as 3rd except
  7½" x 5"......................$30.00 – 35.00

3rd Row:
Colonial Couple Seated.....$30.00 – 35.00
Man with Urn ....$30.00 – 40.00
Colonial Pair ....$40.00 – 45.00

Page 167
Top Row:
1st & 2nd Double Pair,
  11" ....$35.00 – 40.00 ea./$70.00 – 80.00 pr.
3rd Couple, 10½" ....$35.00 – 40.00
4th Couple, 10½" ....$40.00 – 45.00
5th Male Bouquet Holder, 10"..$30.00 – 35.00
6th Lady's Head, 10" ....$50.00 – 55.00

2nd Row:
1st & 2nd Double Pair,
  10½"..$35.00 - 40.00 ea./$70.00 – 80.00 pr.
3rd Musician and Singer,
  11½"........................$35.00 – 40.00
4th Dancing Couple, 11½"..$50.00 – 55.00
5th Courting Couple, 10" ...$35.00 – 40.00

3rd Row:
1st and 2nd Pair,
  11" ....$60.00 ea./$100.00 – 120.00 pr.
2nd, 3rd and 4th Couples, 10" and
  11½"..............................$40.00 – 50.00 ea.

Page 168
Top Row:
1st and 2nd, Courting Couple,
  6½"....................$50.00 – 60.00 pr.
3rd, Basket Carrier, 8⅛" ..$30.00 – 35.00
4th, Cowboy, 7⅜" ....$30.00 – 35.00

2nd Row:
1st and 2nd White w/Gold Colonials,
  7⅜"............................$60.00 – 70.00 pr.
3rd, Oriental Reading Book .$30.00 – 35.00

3rd Row:
Pink Hatted Lady, 8⅛" .....$30.00 – 35.00
Seated Bisque Couple.......$65.00 – 75.00
Lady Lifting Skirt..............$30.00 – 35.00

Page 169
Top Row:
"Fleur de lis" design, four 10" square napkins and
  one 32" square tablecloth..$85.00 – 100.00 set

2nd Row:
Damask set of four 12" square napkins and one
  48" x 52" tablecloth....$100.00 – 120.00 set

3rd Row:
Linen set of four 10½" napkins and one 32"
  square tablecloth..........$90.00 – 100.00 set

4th Row:
Tablecloth, 48" square.......$40.00 – 50.00
Tablecloth, 50" x 50" ....$45.00 – 50.00
Four Damask Napkins, 12½"
  square........$12.00 ea. /$50.00 – 52.50 set

5th Row:
Embroidered Towels 13" x 17"..$20.00 – 25.00 ea.
Peach Tablecloth and Napkin
  Set ....$75.00 – 100.00 set
Napkins, 12½" square.......$10.00 – 12.00 ea.

Page 170
Clockwise from top left:
Wool hooked rug, 9' x 12' .$300.00 – 400.00
Wool hooked rug, 3' x 5' .$75.00 – 100.00
Woven rug, 3' x 5' ....$50.00 – 60.00
Wool hooked rug, 4' x 6' ...$75.00 – 76.00

Page 171
Top Row:
Silk Scarf, 48" x 18½" ......$50.00 – 60.00
Baby Sweater ....$40.00 – 50.00
Cat Pincushion, 3½" x 5¼" ..$12.50 – 15.00

2nd Row:
Organdy Crewel Scarf,
  11" x 5¼".......................$20.00 – 25.00

3rd Row:
Lamp Scarves, 10¾" square..$25.00 – 27.50 ea.

4th Row:
Celluloid Tape Measure, 3" Girl ..$15.00 – 20.00
Heart Box ....$4.00 – 5.00
Sewing Kit.........................$18.00 – 20.00
Picture, "Omi Art Embroidery
  Co."...............................$45.00 – 50.00

Page 172
Top Row:
Lamp Lighter ....$17.50 – 20.00
Donkey Lighter..................$20.00 – 22.50
Boot Lighter ....$6.00 – 8.00

2nd Row:
Coat of Armor Lighter ......$15.00 – 17.50
Inlaid Lighter....................$12.50 – 15.00
Mint Compote ....$5.00 – 6.00
Table Gun Lighter (pearl) ..$20.00 – 22.50
Shoe Pin Cushion.................$7.50 – 8.00

3rd Row:
Table Lighter......................$5.00 – 6.00
Gun Lighter......................$12.00 – 15.00
Bulldog Pencil Sharpener .$10.00 – 12.00
Shaker and Mustard Set
  w/Tray ....$22.50 – 25.00
Trophies ....$2.00 – 2.50
Donkey Jewel Chest ....$17.50 – 20.00

Bottom:
Tea Holder ....$15.00 – 18.00
Nut Dish..............................$5.00 – 6.00

Key Lighter ....$12.00 – 15.00
Pencil Lighter...................$25.00 – 30.00

Page 173
Top Row:
Telephone Cigarette
  Lighters ....$17.50 – 20.00 ea.
Cast Metal Skillet and Handle .$15.00 – 20.00

2nd Row:
Champagne Bottle Lighter..$17.50 – 20.00
Football Lighter ....$12.50 – 15.00
Belt Buckle Lighter ....$35.00 – 40.00

3rd Row:
Letter Opener and Case ...$12.50 – 15.00
Miniature Lighter................$8.00 – 10.00
Miniature Harmonica on Chain .$8.00 – 10.00
Hav-A-Shot, Bullet Carrier &
  Glasses..........................$15.00 – 20.00
Buddha Gods...................$12.50 – 15.00 ea.
Spoon, Desco Stainless.........$2.00 – 3.00
Horse and Rider...............$15.00 – 20.00

Bottom Row:
Pliers in Original Box........$25.00 – 30.00
Wrench in Original Box ....$25.00 – 30.00

Page 174
Top Row:
Sugar and Creamer on a Tray..$15.00 – 20.00
Cowboy Hat Ash Tray
  (5" Width) ....$6.00 – 8.00
Candlestick, Pair..............$15.00 – 20.00
Tumbler (5 oz.) ....$6.00 – 7.50

2nd Row:
Desk Set (Exceptional Quality) .$25.00 – 30.00
Match or Cigarette Holders ......$3.00 – 4.00 ea.

3rd Row:
Piano Jewelry Holder ....$12.00 – 15.00
Candy Container (Handled) .$12.00 – 15.00
Antimony Desk Set ....$25.00 – 30.00

4th Row:
Ash Tray..............................$3.00 – 4.00
Ash Tray, Souvenir of Alaska.$5.00 – 6.00

Page 175
Top Row:
Dragon Mug ("Engraved
  "Sue") ....$15.00 – 20.00
Cigarette Holder ....$3.00 – 4.00
Tea or Spice Canister.......$12.50 – 15.00

2nd Row:
Leaf Candy Dish...............$10.00 – 12.00
Salt & Pepper Shakers.......$8.00 – 10.00 pr.
Salt & Pepper Shakers on
  Tray ....$10.00 – 12.00
Open Candy Dish ....$6.00 – 8.00
Piano Cigarette Dispenser..$20.00 – 25.00

3rd Row:
Jewelry Boxes, 5 Assorted
  Sizes ....$10.00 – 15.00 ea.

Open Candy Dish ....$10.00 – 12.00
Hand Warmer & Chamois Bag ....$30.00 – 35.00
Butter Dish........................$12.50 – 15.00
Sugar & Creamer, Pair.....$12.50 – 15.00

4th Row:
Cowboy Ash Tray................$4.00 – 5.00
Heart Ash Tray (Hot Springs, Ark.) ....$4.00 – 5.00
Cowboy Hat Ash Tray (3" Wide) ....$6.00 – 8.00

Page 176

Vertically from top
Column 1:
Butler, 5¼" x 6"..................$8.00 – 10.00
Copper Butler, souvenir of Washington, D. C. ....$8.00 – 10.00
Butler, NY souvenir..........$12.00 – 15.00
Crumb Butler.........................$6.00 – 8.00
Crumb Butler, souvenir of Washington, D. C. ....$5.00 – 6.00

Column 2:
Tray, 9½" x 4½"...................$8.00 – 9.00
Tray, 4¾" x 2", United Nations souvenir ....$8.00 – 10.00
Bronze Tray, 4¼" x 5¾" ....$6.00 – 7.50
Ash Tray, 4¾" Souvenir of N.Y.C. ....$12.50 – 15.00

Column 3:
Turtle Wind-Up Toy ....$25.00 – 30.00
Puzzles w/mirror on back, 2¼" (Clown, Dog, Cat)............$10.00 – 12.00 ea.

Column 4:
Ash Tray, N.Y.C. souvenir .$10.00 – 12.50
Heart Trays Souvenirs of Canada and New Orleans ....$5.00 – 6.00 ea.
Trays, 5" 3½", souvenirs of New Mexico and Washington, D. C. ....$5.00 – 6.00 ea.

Page 177

Top Row:
Basket..............................$18.00 – 20.00
Floral Vase ....$12.50 – 15.00
Urn Vase ....$10.00 – 12.50
Copper Urn Vase w/Grapes..$12.50 – 15.00
Container w/Lid ....$12.50 – 15.00

2nd Row:
Bird Cage Clock..........$200.00 – 250.00
Bowl w/Three Angel Feet..$12.50 – 15.00
3rd and 4th, Sugar/Creamer Set ....$20.00 – 22.50

3rd Row:
Red Ring Box ....$10.00 – 12.50
Dragon Cigarette Box and Tray ....$15.00 – 20.00
Box ....$10.00 – 12.50

4th Row:
Inkwell w/Pen Holder.......$15.00 – 20.00
Bowl, 4-footed w/Lid........$12.50 – 15.00
Heart Box ....$10.00 – 12.50
Box w/Peacock ....$15.00 – 17.50

5th Row:
Candy Compote ....$10.00 – 12.50
Cowboy Hat and Glove Top..$8.00 – 10.00
Lockable Box ....$12.50 – 15.00
Small Box w/Peacock........$8.00 – 10.00

Page 178

Top Row:
Ash Tray, Alaska ....$10.00 – 12.50
Ash Tray, Colorado ....$2.00 – 3.00
Ash Tray, Chicago ....$2.00 – 3.00
Ash Tray, Leaf w/Grapes ....$2.00 – 3.00
Ash Tray, Washington, D.C. $8.00 – 10.00

2nd Row:
1st, 3rd – 6th, Cigarette Urns..$3.00 – 4.00 ea.
2nd, Creamer ....$8.00 – 10.00
7th, Hand Ash Tray ....$8.00 – 10.00

3rd Row:
1st and 9th, Creamer and Sugar ....$15.00 – 18.00 pr.
2nd – 8th, Gods................$12.50 – 15.00 ea.

4th Row:
1st, San Francisco Trolley ..$20.00 – 22.50
2nd, Small Sugar (Matches Cream in Row 2)...........................$8.00 – 10.00
3rd and 4th, Cigarette Urns ..$3.00 – 4.00 ea.
5th, Creamer ....$10.00 – 12.50
6th – 8th, Saki Glasses or Small Urns ....$4.00 – 6.00 ea.

5th Row:
Pegasus Embossed Box ....$10.00 – 12.00
Crown Embossed Box ....$10.00 – 12.00
Silent Butler ....$15.00 – 20.00
Horse Ash Tray ....$15.00 – 17.50
Pegasus Embossed Box ....$10.00 – 12.00

Page 179

Top Row:
Jewel Box, 3½" x 4½" ......$10.00 – 12.50
2nd and 4th Vase, 8" ....32.50 – 35.00 pr.
3rd Vase, 7" ....$15.00 – 17.50
Cigarette Box, 3½" x 4¼" .$15.00 – 18.00

2nd Row:
1st and 3rd Sugar and Creamer on 7½" Tray ....$20.00 – 25.00 ea.
2nd Miniature Set on 4" Tray .$15.00 – 17.50

3rd Row:
Horse and Sulky...............$25.00 – 27.50
Salt and Pepper on Tray, 5⅜" .$20.00 – 25.00
Handled Candlestick ....$20.00 – 25.00 pr.

4th Row:
1st and 2nd Piano Jewel Boxes, 2½ " x 3" ....$12.00 – 15.00 ea.
Bowl, 6¼" ....$8.00 – 10.00
Piano Box, 2¼" x 3½".......$12.00 – 15.00
Cowboy Boot........................$5.00 – 6.00

5th Row:
Dragon Covered Box, 4" x 7" .$25.00 – 27.50
Salt and Pepper on Tray ..$15.00 – 17.50
Jewel Box, w/Lock, 3¾" x 6¾"......................$25.00 – 30.00

Page 180

Top 2 Rows:
Set of Six Mugs ....$125.00 – 150.00

3rd Row:
Dog Tobies ....$30.00 – 35.00 ea.
Lady................................$10.00 – 12.00
Skull ....$20.00 – 25.00
Devil ....$35.00 – 40.00

4th Row:
1st Toby ....$20.00 – 25.00
2nd Toby ....$25.00 – 30.00
Indian ....$30.00 – 35.00

Page 181

Top Row:
Stein Imitation ....$12.00 – 15.00
Bunny Handled Mug ....$17.50 – 20.00
Endowed Lady Handled Mug..............................$25.00 – 30.00

2nd Row:
1st, 3rd People Handled Mugs ....$15.00 – 20.00 ea.
Bickering Mug (Possibly of Set) ....$20.00 – 25.00

3rd Row:
All Mugs ....$15.00 – 20.00 ea.

4th Row:
Nude Lady Handled Mug .$20.00 – 25.00
Parson Toby...................$75.00 – 100.00
Gentleman Toby ....$25.00 – 30.00

Page 182

Top Row:
Cowboy Mug....................$25.00 – 30.00
Cowboy Mug....................$20.00 – 22.50
Santa Mug ....$30.00 – 35.00
Brown Elephant Mug, 4¾" ..$17.50 – 20.00

2nd Row:
People Mugs ....$15.00 – 20.00 ea.

3rd Row:
Nickel-plated 5" Mugs (made from battleship parts) ....$35.00 – 50.00 ea.

4th Row:
1st, Indian Head Mug ......$12.50 – 15.00
2nd, Small Mug....................$5.00 – 6.00
3rd, Small Mug ....$5.00 – 6.00
4th, Cupids w/Bow...........$12.50 – 15.00

Page 183

Top Row:
All Toby Mugs ....$15.00 – 17.50

''',
2nd Row:
All Toby Mugs Save 3rd from
Left....................$15.00 – 20.00
3rd Toby Mug from Left ....$22.50 – 25.00

3rd Row:
Tobies, either end ....$25.00 – 30.00
Other Toby Mugs............$15.00 – 17.50

4th Row:
Oriental Head Vases.........$50.00 – 60.00
#2 and 4 Small Heads.......$20.00 – 25.00
#3 Large Head ....$25.00 – 30.00

5th Row:
1st Two Toby Mugs...........$12.50 – 15.00
3rd Toby.........................$30.00 – 35.00
Barrel Mug ....$15.00 – 20.00
MacArthur Toby ....$65.00 – 75.00

Page 184

Top Row:
Winker, 4" ....$25.00 – 30.00
Barrel, 4¼" ....$10.00 – 12.00
Cannibal Handled Mug, 4¼"..$35.00 – 40.00

2nd Row:
Bearded Man, 2¾" ....$17.50 – 20.00
Colonial Man, 2¾"..........$15.00 – 17.50
3rd and 5th Colonial Lady,
2" ....$12.50 ea./$27.50 – 30.00 pr.
Old Man, 1¾" ....$12.50 – 15.00
Lady w/Basket, 2¼" ....$12.50 – 15.00
Lady w/Fork, 2¾"............$15.00 – 17.50
Red Bearded Man, 2⅞"....$17.50 – 20.00

3rd Row:
1st and 2nd Scarf Lady,
2½"..........................$35.00 – 37.50 pr.
3rd Mustache Man, 2¼" ...$25.00 – 27.50
4th and 6th Lady, 2½"......$20.00 – 22.50
5th Colonial Man, 3¼".......$20.00 – 25.00

4th Row:
Stein, 6¾" ....$17.50 – 20.00
Stein, 7⅛" ....$20.00 – 22.50
Bearded Man, 4" ....$25.00 – 30.00

5th Row:
Father Cup and Saucer
Set ....$25.00 – 30.00 ea.

Page 185

Top Row:
Toby Pitcher, barkeep holding two mugs
4⅞"..........................$40.00 – 50.00
Steins, three musketeers
partying ....$22.50 – 25.00
Winker Pitcher ....$25.00 – 30.00

2nd Row:
Toby w/Mustache ....$30.00 – 35.00

Individual Teapot, 3⅝" .....$35.00 – 40.00
Toby Pitcher, 4⅞".............$30.00 – 35.00

3rd Row:
Stein, Man and Woman w/Dog,
8½".............................$35.00 – 40.00
Mug w/Coach Scene ....$12.50 – 15.00
Stein...............................$30.00 – 35.00

4th Row:
Mug w/Fishermen ....$12.50 – 15.00
Pitcher, 3" ....$15.00 – 20.00
Pitcher, 2" ....$12.50 – 15.00
Pitcher.............................$20.00 – 25.00
Pitcher.............................$20.00 – 25.00

Page 186

Top Row:
Boy at Cactus, 4" ....$6.00 – 8.00
Girl w/Fan, 6" ....$12.50 – 15.00
Chinese Pair of Planters, 5" ....$10.00 ea.
Seated Oriental, 4" ....$8.00 – 10.00

2nd Row:
Dancers, 4½" ....$15.00 – 20.00 ea.
Colonial Lady, 4"..................$5.00 – 6.00
Oriental Lady Head, 4"....$12.50 – 15.00
Girl Pushing Cart, 4".........$10.00 – 12.50

3rd Row:
Boy w/Bird, 3" ....$5.00 – 6.00
Couple, 2½" ....$8.00 – 10.00
Boy w/Flowers, 2"...............$3.00 – 4.00
Boy w/Horn, 3" ....$8.00 – 10.00
Boy w/Guitar, 2¾"...............$6.00 – 8.00
Dutch Girl w/Cart, 2¾" ....$8.00 – 10.00

4th Row:
Girl w/White Dress, 7" (Florence
Ceramics copy) ....$20.00 – 25.00
Boy w/Hat, 5½" ....$10.00 – 12.50
Coolie w/Basket, 6"..........$10.00 – 12.50
Elf w/Cart, 7½".................$15.00 – 20.00
Oriental, 5½"...................$15.00 – 17.50

5th Row:
Mexican w/Guitar, 4¼" ....$15.00 – 17.50
Sleepy Mexican, 3½" ....$10.00 – 12.50
Mandolin Player, 4".............$6.00 – 8.00
Boy w/Topknot, 4" ....$12.50 – 15.00
Girl w/Basket, 4¾" ....$10.00 – 12.50

Page 187

Top Row:
1st and 2nd, Oriental Girl and Boy,
4⅛"...........................$7.50 – 10.00 ea.
3rd, Head Vase ....$20.00 – 22.00
4th and 5th, Oriental Boy and Girl,
5"..............................$12.50 – 15.00 ea.
6th, Big Hat Oriental, 5⅛" ....$6.00 – 8.00
7th, Shelf Sitter Planter.....$12.50 – 15.00

2nd Row:
1st, Seated Mandolin Player .$6.00 – 8.00

2nd and 3rd, Boy
w/Rickshaw.................$10.00 – 12.50 ea.
4th, Oriental Couple ....$15.00 – 17.50
5th, Carriage Boy ....$5.00 – 6.00

3rd Row:
Heart w/Angel, 3⅝".........$10.00 – 12.00
Umbrella Girl.....................$8.00 – 10.00
Chicken Feeding Boy..........$8.00 – 10.00
Girl Reading Book ....$8.00 – 10.00
Girl w/Accordion ....$4.00 – 5.00
Colonial Man, 4⅝"...........$10.00 – 12.50

4th Row:
1st and 2nd, Dutch Boy and Girl,
4½".............................$15.00 – 18.00 ea.
3rd, Girl, matches 6th in row
above ....$10.00 – 12.50
4th, Couple.........................$5.00 – 6.00
5th, Girl w/Urn....................$5.00 – 6.00
6th, Boy playing Ukulele ....$8.00 – 10.00

5th Row:
1st and 2nd, Boy and Girl on Fence
w/Dog, 4¾" ....$8.00 – 10.00 ea.
3rd, Dutch Girl w/Buckets ..$8.00 – 10.00
4th, Girl w/Duck, 4⅝" ....$8.00 – 10.00
5th, Sleepy Mexican.............$8.00 – 10.00

Page 188

Top Row:
Oriental Girl w/Fan Planter,
6⅛".............................$10.00 – 12.50
Man with Vase.....................$5.00 – 6.00
Man with Bucket Planters,
6¾"............................$20.00 – 22.50
Girl Musician Planter ....$6.00 – 8.00
Oriental Man, matches 1st
Girl...............................$10.00 – 12.50

2nd Row:
Boy Skier Planter, 3⅜", and Girl
w/Book.........................$6.00 – 8.00 ea.
Girl on Bench ....$8.00 – 10.00
Boy Planter.........................$6.00 – 8.00
Oriental Boy w/Basket and Matching
Girl.............................$6.00 – 8.00 ea.

3rd Row:
1st and 2nd, Boy and Girl w/Cart,
2⅝".............................$5.00 – 6.00 ea.
3rd and 4th, Boy and Girl at
Well.............................$5.00 – 6.00 ea.
5th, Two Children w/Wheeled Cart
Planter ....$6.00 – 8.00
6th, Boy w/Horn Planter ....$6.00 – 8.00

4th Row:
Boy w/Rickshaw Planter...$10.00 – 12.50
Oriental Girl w/Fan Planter..$10.00 – 12.00
Girl w/Dog Planter, 4⅝" ...$10.00 – 12.00
Boy Musician Planter ....$8.00 – 10.00
Dutch Boy Planter...............$8.00 – 10.00
Boy w/Cart Planter............$8.00 – 10.00

Price Guide →

5th Row:
Musician w/Dog Planter, 4⅛" .$10.00 – 12.50
Man Walking Donkey Cart
    Planter ....$6.00 – 8.00
Boy w/Lamb Planter, 5"....$12.50 – 15.00
Girl w/Goose Planter ....$5.00 – 6.00
Girl w/Basket Planter ....$5.00 – 6.00
Oriental w/Large Hat Planter..$7.50 – 10.00

Page 189
Top Row:
Oriental Girl w/Shell Planter,
    6⅛"..........................$22.50 – 25.00
Tulip Gal Planter.................$8.00 – 10.00
Large Hatted Girl Planter.$12.50 – 15.00
Rickshaw Boy Planter.......$12.50 – 15.00

2nd Row:
Accordion Player w/Dog Planter,
    4⅛"..........................$10.00 – 12.50
Lady Planter ....$5.00 – 6.00
Girl w/Dried Floral
    Arrangement ....$6.00 – 8.00
Dutch Couple Planter..........$8.00 – 10.00
Girl w/Dog Planter.............$8.00 – 10.00
Couple on Bench Planter ....$8.00 – 10.00
Child Playing Violin on Fence
    Planter ....$8.00 – 10.00

3rd Row:
Girl w/Mandolin Planter,
    3⅝"...............................$8.00 – 10.00
Girl w/Horse Cart Planter ....$5.00 – 6.00
Girl w/Basket Planter ....$8.00 – 10.00
Duck Chasing Girl at Wall
    Planter ....$10.00 – 12.50
Dutch Guy Planter ....$10.00 – 12.50
Matching Dutch Girl Planter..$10.00 – 12.50

4th Row:
1st and 2nd, Girl w/Shell Planter,
    2¾".............................$6.00 – 8.00 ea.
3rd, Oriental Boy w/Basket..$5.00 – 6.00
4th, Boy on Fence ....$8.00 – 10.00
5th, Colonial w/Basket ....$5.00 – 6.00
6th, Mexican Planter............$5.00 – 9.00
7th, Napping Musician..........$6.00 – 8.00

5th Row:
Boy w/Cherry Tree, 3⅝".....$8.00 – 10.00
Shepherd Planter ....$8.00 – 10.00
Boy w/Bird Planter...............$6.00 – 8.00
Boy w/Fiddle ....$6.00 – 8.00
Umbrella Boy ....$8.00 – 10.00
Red Hooded Lady Planter, 4⅝"..$8.00 – 10.00

Page 190
Top Row:
Rectangular Relief, Bisque (probably one of
    a pair)............................$40.00 – 45.00

2nd Row:
Round Relief Musical Couple,
    Bisque ....$35.00 – 40.00 ea.

Pair ....$60.00 – 80.00
Swingers Relief ....$25.00 – 30.00 ea.
    Pair ....$50.00 – 60.00

3rd Row:
Heads, Crinoline Lined......$20.00 – 25.00 ea.
    Pair ....$40.00 – 50.00
Standing Colonials, Relief .$20.00 – 25.00 ea.
    Pair ....$40.00 – 50.00

4th Row:
Fall and Spring Plaques .....$8.00 – 10.00 ea.

Page 191
Top Row:
Japanese Pair, Chalkware..$25.00 – 30.00 ea.
    Pair ....$50.00 – 60.00
Oriental Bisque, Relief......$25.00 – 30.00 ea.
    Pair ....$50.00 – 60.00

2nd Row:
Iris Wall Pocket ....$20.00 – 22.00
Dutch Pair, Chalkware......$25.00 – 30.00 ea.
    Pair ....$50.00 – 60.00
Cupped Saucer ....$8.00 – 10.00

Page 192
Top Row:
Colonial Couple, 6½" x 6"..$45.00 – 50.00
Couple similar to one above ..$45.00 – 50.00
Colonial Lady, 7" x 4¾" ...$25.00 – 30.00

2nd Row:
Colonial Couple,
    6½" x 5¾" ...$40.00 ea./$80.00 – 85.00 pr.
Dutch Boy, 7½"................$20.00 – 25.00

3rd Row:
Couple w/Baskets,
    6⅞" x 4¾" .$45.00 ea./$95.00 – 100.00 pr.
Monkeys, 5" ....$35.00 – 40.00 ea.

Page 193
Top Row:
Chicken and Girl ....$8.00 – 9.00 ea.
Boats /3 Piece Sets ....$17.50 – 20.00
    Gaily Decorated ....$20.00 – 25.00

2nd Row:
4 Piece Metal Set ....$20.00 – 25.00
Glass Shakers and Metal
    Stand ....$20.00 – 25.00
Hobnail Shakers...............$17.50 – 20.00 pr.
Frogs/3 Piece Set............$20.00 – 25.00
Clown ....$15.00 – 20.00

3rd Row:
Tomato, Pr. ....$10.00 – 12.00
Tomato Sets on Leaf
    w/Mustard ....$25.00 – 30.00

4th Row:
Blue/White Shakers ....$20.00 – 25.00 pr.
Windmills w/Moving Blades .$25.00 – 30.00 pr.

Black Cooks, pr. ....$40.00 – 50.00 pr.
Cottages and Peppers........$10.00 – 12.00
Boy ....$8.00 – 9.00

5th Row:
Beehive Set......................$25.00 – 30.00
Beehive Sugar and Marmalade...$20.00 –
25.00
Separate Sugar ....$10.00 – 12.50
Ceramic Set on Tray........$20.00 – 25.00

Page 194
Top Row:
1st, Cobalt Blue Shakers, Mustard with
    Spoon on Tray..............$45.00 – 50.00
2nd, Urns w/Tray.............$20.00 – 22.50
3rd, Cobalt Blue Set ....$45.00 – 50.00

2nd Row:
Coffee Pot Set..................$12.50 – 15.00
Skillet, flowers on tray ......$20.00 – 22.50
Urns on Tray....................$15.00 – 17.50
Teapots on Tray ....$15.00 – 17.50
Penguins..........................$20.00 – 22.50

3rd Row:
Tall Gold Colored Shakers ...$15.00 – 17.50
Box and Shakers to its right..$20.00 – 22.50 set

4th Row:
Cocktail Shakers on Tray..$20.00 – 22.50
Single Elephant................$10.00 – 12.50
Single Urn........................$5.00 – 6.00
Souvenir Shakers ....$12.50 – 15.00
Candles on Tray...............$20.00 – 22.50
Single Coffee Pot ....$6.00 – 8.00

5th Row:
Cowboy Boots ....$12.50 – 15.00
Egg Set: Cup and Shakers..$25.00 – 30.00
Lamp Set ....$15.00 – 20.00
Ship..................................$22.50 – 25.00
Single Donkey Loaded
    w/Tools..........................$10.00 – 12.50

Page 195
Top Row:
1st, Clown Crouching on Drum..$40.00 – 45.00
2nd, Clown on Back on Drum ..$40.00 – 45.00
3rd and 4th, Cat Pair........$15.00 – 17.50
5th and 6th, Hat Pair ....$12.50 – 15.00 pr.

2nd Row:
1st, Six-piece Colonial Scene
    Set ....$25.00 – 30.00 set
2nd and 3rd, Dutch Couple .$12.50 – 15.00 pr.
4th, Three-piece Flowers on
    Basket..........................$15.00 – 20.00

3rd Row:
1st and 2nd, Totem Pole Set..$10.00 – 12.50 pr.
3rd and 4th, Mugs............$12.50 – 15.00 pr.
5th and 6th, Pigs ....$15.00 – 20.00 pr.
7th and 8th, Squirrels........$12.50 – 15.00 pr.

4th Row:
(Single prices given, double price for pair)
Toadstool .... $6.00 – 8.00
Mexican Lady .... $6.00 – 8.00
"Hummel-like" Boy .... $6.00 – 8.00
Dutch Girl .... $6.00 – 8.00
Boy w/Lederhosen .... $5.00 – 6.00
Geisha w/Fan .... $8.00 – 10.00
"Hummel-like" Boy, 4⅜" ...... $8.00 – 10.00
Bird .... $5.00 – 6.00
Dutch Boy Bust .... $6.00 – 8.00

5th Row:
Toby Winker .... $10.00 – 12.50
Popeye .... $30.00 – 40.00
Duck .... $5.00 – 6.00
Dutch Girl .... $6.00 – 8.00
Cowboy .... $8.00 – 10.00
Strawberry .... $5.00 – 6.00
Seated Dutch Girl .... $6.00 – 8.00
Paddling Indian .... $6.00 – 8.00

Page 196

Top Row:
Humpty Dumpty .... $55.00 – 60.00 pr.
Humpty Dumpty, small .... $30.00 – 35.00 pr.
Mammy and Pappy .... $40.00 – 50.00

2nd Row:
Chicks in Basket .... $20.00 – 22.50
"Hummel"-type Children ..... $17.50 – 20.00
Chickens in Basket .... $20.00 – 22.50
Mammy and Pappy .... $40.00 – 50.00

3rd Row:
Pigs .... $15.00 – 20.00
Pigs in Sty .... $20.00 – 25.00
Dogs .... $12.50 – 15.00
Southern Belles .... $12.50 – 15.00

4th Row:
Indians .... $15.00 – 17.50
Indians in Canoe .... $22.50 – 25.00
Fat Boy .... $6.00 – 8.00
Boy w/Suspenders .... $6.00 – 8.00
Duck Hugger .... $10.00 – 12.00

5th Row:
Corn Cobs .... $10.00 – 12.50
Deer .... $12.50 – 15.00
Pitchers on Tray .... $20.00 – 22.50

6th Row:
1st and 5th Geese pairs . $15.00 – 17.50 ea pr.
2nd Duck .... $10.00 – 12.50 pr.
3rd Ducks and 4th Geese
    pairs .... $12.50 – 15.00 ea pr.

Page 197

Top Row:
Baseball Players .... $25.00 – 30.00
Geisha Girls .... $18.00 – 20.00
Bellhop .... $20.00 – 25.00
Coolies .... $27.50 – 30.00

2nd Row:
Graduates .... $18.00 – 20.00
Bride and Groom (Before &
    After) .... $25.00 – 30.00
Scottish Couple .... $15.00 – 17.50
Dutch Girls .... $15.00 – 17.50

3rd Row:
Indian Zither Players .... $15.00 – 17.50
Basket Children .... $20.00 – 22.50
Lily of the Valley .... $12.50 – 15.00
Teakettles .... $10.00 – 12.50
Teakettle, single .... $6.00 – 7.50

4th Row:
Cottage and Lighthouse ..... $22.50 – 25.00
Children w/Animals .... $30.00 – 35.00
Glass Shakers on Tray ..... $30.00 – 35.00

5th Row:
Glass on Metal Tray .... $17.50 – 20.00
Metal Shakers on Tray ..... $15.00 – 17.50
Lady Mustard, Shakers,
    Spoon .... $40.00 – 45.00

Page 198

Top Row:
All Items Save Windmills, Miniature Toby
    Shakers .... $12.00 – 15.00 pr.
Windmills and Toby .... $15.00 – 17.50 pr.

2nd Row:
All Items Save Martha and
    George .... $12.00 – 15.00 pr.
Martha and George .... $20.00 – 25.00 pr.

3rd Row:
All Items Save Frogs and
    Rabbits .... $10.00 – 12.00 pr.
Frogs and Rabbits .... $25.00 – 30.00 pr.

4th Row:
Three Piece Sets .... $20.00 – 25.00 ea.

5th Row:
Three Piece Sets, Save
    Cucumbers .... $25.00 – 30.00
Cucumbers .... $30.00 – 35.00

Page 199

Top Row:
Fruit Shakers (3 Part) .... $15.00 – 20.00
Fireside Shakers (5 Part, Includes
    Mustard) .... $30.00 – 35.00
Flowers (3 Part) .... $25.00 – 30.00

2nd Row:
Cats and Birds .... $12.00 – 15.00 pr.
Dutch Children .... $15.00 – 20.00 pr.

3rd Row:
1st, 2nd Pairs .... $8.00 – 10.00 pr.
Strawberry Set (3 Part) .... $15.00 – 20.00
Toby Mug Type .... $20.00 – 25.00 pr.

4th Row:
Bears, Hugging .... $20.00 – 25.00
All Other Pairs .... $10.00 – 12.50 pr.

5th Row:
All Pairs .... $10.00 – 12.50 pr.

Page 200

Top Row – Strawberry:
Sugar w/Lid and Creamer on
    Tray .... $25.00 – 30.00 set
Salt, Pepper, Mustard
    w/Spoon .... $25.00 – 30.00 set

2nd Row – Tomato:
Salt and Pepper, 3½" .... $17.50 – 20.00
Salt and Pepper, 3" .... $15.00 – 17.50
Sugar w/Lid .... $12.50 – 15.00

3rd Row – Tomato:
Salt, Pepper, and Mustard . $20.00 – 25.00 set
Teapot, 3" .... $30.00 – 35.00
Tumbler, 3" .... $10.00 – 12.50

4th Row – Tomato:
Teapot, 4½" .... $40.00 – 45.00
Teapot, 5½" .... $50.00 – 55.00
Tumbler as in Row 3

5th Row – Tomato:
Tumbler as in Row 3
Sugar w/Lid and Creamer .. $25.00 – 30.00
Salt, Pepper, and Mustard
    w/Spoon .... $27.50 – 30.00 set

Page 201

Top Row:
Honeycomb Design Creamer,
    2⅝" .... $12.50 – 15.00
Sugar w/Lid to match .... $20.00 – 22.50
Beehive Teapot w/Honeycomb
    Design .... $35.00 – 40.00
Beehive Honey Jar .... $22.50 – 25.00
Bee Two-part Relish .... $17.50 – 20.00

2nd Row:
1st, Honeycomb Creamer, 2¾" . $12.50 – 15.00
2nd – 4th, Three-piece Set . $20.00 – 22.50 set
5th, Marmalade Hive .... $15.00 – 17.50
6th, Honeycomb Design Sugar
    w/Lid .... $20.00 – 22.50
7th, Honeycomb Design Honey
    Jar .... $22.50 – 25.00
8th, Salt and Pepper
    w/Holder .... $15.00 – 17.50 set

3rd Row:
1st, Cottage Creamer, 2⅝" .. $12.50 – 15.00
2nd, Cottage Creamer, 2" .. $10.00 – 12.50
3rd, Large Sugar to match 1st
    creamer .... $22.50 – 25.00
4th and 5th, Salt and
    Pepper .... $17.50 – 20.00 pr.

6th, Sugar to match 2nd
    creamer ....$15.00 – 17.50

4th Row:
Tomato Sugar ....$15.00 – 17.50
Tomato Cracker or Biscuit Jar .$75.00 – 85.00
Tomato Sugar ....$15.00 – 17.50

Page 202

Top Row:
Three-piece Toby Set .....$85.00 – 100.00

2nd Row:
Windmill Sugar, 4" ....$17.50 – 20.00
Windmill Creamer, 3" ....$10.00 – 12.00
Windmill Large Salt, 3" .....$10.00 – 12.00
Windmill Teapot, 5" ....$40.00 – 50.00

3rd Row:
Salt, Pepper, and Marmalade on
    Tray ....$30.00 – 35.00
Salt, Pepper, and Mustard on
    Tray ....$25.00 – 30.00
Sugar w/Lid....................$17.50 – 20.00

4th Row:
Cookie Jar, 8" x 6¼" ....$75.00 – 90.00
Cottage Grease or Sugar .$15.00 – 20.00
Biscuit Jar, 6½" x 5¼" ......$55.00 – 70.00

5th Row:
Bee Creamer, 2½" ....$12.50 – 15.00
Bee Teapot, 4½" ....$35.00 – 40.00
Bee Sugar w/Lid, 3½" ......$20.00 – 22.50

Page 203

Top Row:
1st, Strawberry Salt and Pepper on
    Tray ....$20.00 – 25.00
2nd and 4th, Strawberry Shakers,
    3⅝"..........................$20.00 – 22.50
3rd, Strawberry Covered
    Sugar ....$17.50 – 20.00
4th, Windmill Teapot..........$40.00 – 50.00

2nd Row:
Windmill Small Creamer, 2⅝"..$10.00 – 12.00
Windmill Sugar w/Lid, 3⅞"..$17.50 – 20.00
Windmill Teapot, 4⅞" ....$40.00 – 50.00
Windmill Large Creamer, 2⅞"..$10.00 – 12.00
Salt and Pepper Set ....$15.00 – 20.00

3rd Row:
Set, salt, pepper and mustard on
    tray...........................$30.00 – 35.00
Covered Dish ....$30.00 – 35.00
Butter Dish......................$35.00 – 40.00
4th – 7th, Butter Pats........$10.00 – 12.50 ea.

4th Row:
Teapot...........................$50.00 – 65.00
Cookie or Biscuit Jar ......$90.00 – 100.00
Sugar and Creamer on Tray .$30.00 – 35.00

Page 204

Top Row:
Creamer ....$8.00 – 10.00
Corn Sugar w/Lid............$12.50 – 15.00
Corn Creamer ....$8.00 – 10.00
Corn Marmalade..............$12.50 – 15.00
Flower Basket Cookie Jar..$20.00 – 25.00

2nd Row:
Rice Bowl ....$6.00 – 8.00
Tea Cup ....$6.00 – 8.00
Corn Marmalade..............$17.50 – 20.00
Tea Cup, bird scene ....$7.50 – 10.00
Rice Bowl, floral.................$5.00 – 6.00
Orange Marmalade ....$12.50 – 15.00

3rd Row:
Pink Lily of Valley Sugar...$12.50 – 15.00
Soup Spoon ....$10.00 – 12.50
Corn Container...................$4.00 – 5.00
Fruit Basket ....$20.00 – 22.50
Basket Weave Butter Dish..$17.50 – 20.00
Egg Cup ....$8.00 – 10.00

4th Row:
1st, Saki Cup in front ....$5.00 – 6.00
2nd, Ship Rice Bowl ....$6.00 – 8.00
3rd, 5th, 7th and 9th, Saki Cups.$5.00 – 6.00 ea.
4th Dragon Rice Bowl.........$8.00 – 10.00
6th, Large Rice Bowl..........$8.00 – 10.00
8th, Red Floral Rice Bowl....$8.00 – 10.00
10th, Large Rice Bowl........$8.00 – 10.00

5th Row:
Iris Small Creamer...........$10.00 – 12.50
Small 4-footed Floral Oval Bowl .$5.00 – 6.00
Saki Cup...........................$5.00 – 6.00
Lobster Sugar w/Lid........$35.00 – 40.00
Lobster Creamer ....$20.00 – 25.00
Lobster 3-part Tray ....$40.00 – 50.00

Page 205

Top Row:
Accordion Boy, 4"............$12.50 – 15.00 ea.
Girl w/Bucket, 3" ....$12.50 – 15.00
Oriental Pair,
    2¾" ....$12.50 ea./$25.00 – 30.00 pr.
Fishing Couple, 2½" ....$15.00 – 17.50

2nd Row:
Musicians, 4½" .$12.50 ea./$25.00 – 30.00 pr.
Oriental Musicians,
    5" ....$15.00 ea./$30.00 – 35.00 pr.
Fishing Couple 4" ....$20.00 – 22.50
Fishing Couple, 2¼" ....$15.00 – 17.50

3rd Row:
Boy with Basket, 4"..........$12.50 – 15.00
2nd and 4th Oriental Pair,
    3" ....$8.50 ea./$17.00 – 20.00 pr.
3rd and 5th Oriental Pair,
    3¼" ....$10.00 ea./$25.00 – 22.50 pr.
Cowboy Couple, 3½" and
    3¾" ....$12.50 ea./$25.00 – 30.00 pr.

Colonial Musicians,
    3¼" ....$11.00 ea./$22.00 – 25.00 pr.

4th Row:
1st and 6th Angels,
    3" ....$20.00 ea./$40.00 – 45.00 pr.
Girl and Doll, 5" ....$17.50 – 20.00
Fishing Boy, 6½" ....$22.50 – 25.00
Ballerina, 5" ....$22.50 – 25.00
Mandolin Player, 4"..........$12.50 – 15.00

Page 206

Top Row:
Bisque Fisherman, 5" ....$17.50 – 20.00
Bisque Fisherman, ...$12.50 – 15.00
Bisque Fisherman, ...$12.50 – 15.00
Book Reader....................$25.00 – 30.00
5th and 6th, Oriental
    Pair. ....$12.50 ea./$25.00 – 30.00 pr.

2nd Row:
1st, Girl w/Red Hat ....$17.50 – 20.00
2nd, Boy Holding Hat ....$12.50 – 15.00
3rd and 4th, Colonial
    Couple..........$8.50 ea./$17.00 – 20.00 pr.
5th, Dutch Girl................$12.50 – 15.00
6th, Dutch Boy ....$12.50 – 15.00
7th, Girl w/Song Book .....$12.50 – 15.00

3rd Row:
Boy w/Horn, 3¾" ....$10.00 – 12.50
Oriental Boy ....$12.50 – 15.00
Girl w/Ruffles...................$17.50 – 20.00
Girl w/Doll, 5" ....$17.50 – 20.00
Bisque Couple ....$12.50 – 15.00
Girl w/Flowers ....$10.00 – 12.50
Boy Playing Banjo ....$8.00 – 10.00

4th Row:
Ballerina, 6⅛" ....$35.00 – 40.00
Boy ....$10.00 – 12.50
Oriental Playing Mandolin.$10.00 – 12.50
Oriental Playing Mandolin...$8.00 – 10.00
Oriental...........................$8.00 – 10.00
Blue Boy ....$8.00 – 10.00

5th Row:
Girl in Green Dress, 3⅝".....$8.00 – 10.00
Girl w/Instrument ....$10.00 – 12.50
Girl w/Music Book ....$15.00 – 17.50
Oriental w/Musical Instrument$10.00 – 12.50
Bisque Cowgirl.................$12.50 – 15.00

Page 207

Top Row:
Dragon Creamer ....$15.00 – 17.50
Dragon Sugar w/Lid.........$25.00 – 27.50
Dragon Demitasse Cup and
    Saucer ....$17.50 – 20.00
Flat Bottomed Cup ....$12.50 – 15.00
Dragon Demitasse Pot ....$85.00 – 100.00
Seventeen-piece set as
    shown ....$235.00 – 265.00

2nd Row:

Teapot, blue trimmed floral ..$30.00 – 35.00

Teapot, floral ....$45.00 – 50.00

Embossed Dragon Teapot .$100.00 – 125.00

Dragon Teapot ....$85.00 – 100.00

3rd Row:

1st and 5th, Floral Demitasse Cup and

    Saucer ....$12.50 – 15.00 set

2nd, Floral Creamer..........$15.00 – 17.50

3rd, Demitasse Pot............$65.00 – 75.00

4th, Floral Sugar w/Lid ....$22.50 – 27.50

Seventeen-piece set as

    shown ....$190.00 – 215.00

4th Row:

Brown Teapot w/Embossed

    Flowers.....................$25.00 – 30.00

Brown Individual Teapot ..$20.00 – 22.50

Blue Stoneware Teapot w/Bamboo

    Handle.........................$25.00 – 30.00

Brown Teapot w/Embossed

    Flowers.....................$30.00 – 35.00

Page 208

Top Row:

1st, Luster Ware Floral Demitasse

    Set ....$10.00 – 12.50

2nd, Tea Set for Six........$75.00 – 100.00

Creamer ....$8.00 – 10.00

Sugar w/Lid.....................$10.00 – 12.50

Teapot................................$30.00 – 35.00

Cup and Saucer (not pictured) .$6.00 – 7.00

2nd Row:

Pink Floral Set for Six ..$200.00 – 250.00

Creamer ....$10.00 – 12.50

Sugar w/Lid.....................$17.50 – 20.00

Teapot................................$65.00 – 75.00

Cup and Saucer................$12.50 – 15.00

Plate....................................$8.00 – 10.00

3rd Row:

Floral w/Ivy Set for Four ..$100.00 – 125.00

Creamer ....$8.00 – 10.00

Sugar w/Lid.....................$12.50 – 15.00

Teapot................................$40.00 – 45.00

Cup and Saucer................$10.00 – 12.00

4th Row:

Demitasse Set ....$8.00 – 10.00

Sugar w/Lid.....................$10.00 – 12.50

Red Bird Teapot ....$35.00 – 40.00

Demitasse Cup/Saucer ....$8.00 – 9.00

Set for Six w/Stand ....$50.00 – 60.00

Individual Teapot..............$12.50 – 15.00

Page 209

Top Row:

1st and 5th, Plate,

    "Noritake"...............$10.00 – 12.50 ea.

2nd, Creamer, "Noritake" ..$17.50 – 20.00

3rd, Teapot, "Noritake" .....$55.00 – 60.00

4th, Sugar w/Lid, "Noritake" .$25.00 – 27.50

2nd Row:

1st and 3rd, Cup and Saucer to match 1st

    row ....$12.50 – 15.00 ea.

2nd, Floral Teapot............$30.00 – 35.00

3rd Row:

Sugar w/Lid.....................$30.00 – 35.00

Teapot w/Lid..................$85.00 – 100.00

Creamer ....$20.00 – 25.00

4th Row:

1st, Brown Two-cup Teapot..$12.00 – 15.00

2nd – 8th, Rust Dragon Saki

    Set ....$100.00 – 125.00

Saki Cup w/Lithopane Geisha

    Girl ....$10.00 – 12.50 ea.

Saki Bottle Only..............$40.00 – 45.00

9th, Brown Teapot ....$10.00 – 12.50

Page 210

Top Row:

Demitasse Set ....$125.00 – 150.00

Cup and Saucer..............$10.00 – 12.50 ea.

Teapot................................$60.00 – 75.00

2nd Row:

Gray Teapot.....................$30.00 – 35.00

Demitasse Cup and Saucer.$8.00 – 10.00

Rust w/Floral Teapot ....$20.00 – 25.00

3rd Row:

Demitasse Set ....$155.00 – 180.00

Cup and Saucer..............$10.00 – 12.50 ea.

Creamer ....$12.50 – 15.00

Sugar w/Lid.....................$17.50 – 20.00

Teapot................................$60.00 – 70.00

4th Row:

Brown Glaze Individual Teapot .$10.00 – 12.50

Brown Glazed Teapot w/Floral

    Design ....$18.00 – 20.00

Individual Brown Glaze Teapot

    w/Lid.............................$6.00 – 8.00

Page 211

Top Row:

Creamer ....$8.00 – 10.00

Rice Bowl, 4" ....$3.00 – 4.00

Bowl, 3" ....$3.00 – 4.00

Rice Bowls, 4½" and 3½" .....$4.00 – 5.00

2nd Row:

Saki Cups, 2¼" ....$6.00 – 7.50 ea.

3rd to 5th and all of Row 3 ..$60.00 – 75.00 set

4th Row:

Demitasse Set for Six........$60.00 – 75.00 set

2nd, 3rd, and 5th Saki Cups,

    2¼"...............................$6.00 – 7.50 ea.

Teapot, 6½" x 9" ....$18.00 – 20.00

Page 212

Top Row:

Sugar, Left.......................$15.00 – 17.50

Teapot, Sugar, and

    Creamer ....$100.00 – 125.00

Individual Teapot.............$15.00 – 17.50

2nd Row:

As Shown ....$125.00 – 150.00

3rd Row:

Creamer and Sugar ....$20.00 – 25.00

Teapot................................$17.50 – 20.00

Page 213

Top Row:

Tea Set ....$75.00 – 85.00

Middle:

Bowl.................................$35.00 – 40.00

Square Flat Dish..............$18.00 – 20.00

Bottom:

Cup and Saucer Set

    w/Stand ....$90.00 – 110.00

Candy Dish ....$15.00 – 17.50

Page 214

Top Row:

Creamer ....$10.00 – 12.00

Toby Teapot ....$50.00 – 60.00

2nd Row:

Floral Creamers ....$15.00 – 17.50 ea.

Sugar, Creamer on Tray ...$30.00 – 35.00

3rd Row:

Sugar and Creamer Sets ..$30.00 – 35.00

4th Row:

Teapots ....$10.00 – 12.50 ea.

Sugar and Creamer Set....$25.00 – 30.00

Page 215

Top Row:

Sugar w/Lid.....................$15.00 – 17.50

Creamer, floral as on sugar ..$10.00 – 12.50

Sugar w/Lid.....................$15.00 – 17.50

Sugar w/Lid.....................$12.50 – 15.00

Creamer to match..............$8.00 – 10.00

Saucer to match ....$2.00 – 3.00

2nd Row:

Creamer ....$6.00 – 8.00

Sugar w/Lid to match ....$10.00 – 12.50

Berry Bowl ....$4.00 – 5.00

4th, Berry Bowl...................$4.00 – 5.00

3rd Row:

Creamer ....$8.00 – 10.00

Sugar w/Lid to match ....$12.50 – 15.00

Sugar w/Lid.....................$15.00 – 17.50

Sugar w/Lid.....................$12.50 – 15.00

Creamer to match..............$8.00 – 10.00

4th Row:

Creamer, small flowers ......$10.00 – 12.50

Sugar w/Lid.....................$17.50 – 20.00
Creamer to match.............$10.00 – 12.50
Cup ....$4.00 – 5.00
Creamer..............................$8.00 – 10.00

5th Row:
Snack Sets.....................$12.50 – 15.00 ea.
Snack Plate ....$5.00 – 6.00

Page 216
Top Row:
Dancing Elephant in Original
    Box ....$75.00 – 100.00
Dancing Bear in Original Box..$50.00 – 65.00
Hopping Squirrel in Original
    Box ....$75.00 – 100.00
    Deduct $25.00 if without box.

2nd Row:
Running Mouse in Original
    Box ....$35.00 – 50.00
Wind-Up Car...............$100.00 – 125.00
Baby Jeep in Box ....$75.00 – 100.00

3rd Row:
Car w/Box....................$100.00 – 125.00
Fly Pin on Card ....$4.50 – 5.00
Beetle.................................$30.00 – 40.00
Watches on Card ....$10.00 – 15.00 ea.

Bottom:
Box of Puzzles
    w/Instructions ....$75.00 – 100.00

Page 217
Top Row:
"Horse and Cart" w/box .$100.00 – 125.00

2nd Row:
"Singing Chicken" w/box ...$40.00 – 50.00
"Sharp Shooter" w/box....$85.00 – 100.00

3rd Row:
"Circus Bear" w/box......$200.00 – 225.00
"Kangaroo" w/box ....$75.00 – 90.00
"Shimmy Donkey" w/box.$100.00 – 125.00

4th Row:
"Lucky Sledge" w/box ....$75.00 – 90.00
"Teddy's Cycle" w/box...$175.00 – 200.00
"Fancy Dan, The Juggling Man"
    w/box ....$175.00 – 200.00

Page 218
Top Row:
1st, "Clever Bear" w/Box..$65.00 – 75.00
2nd and 3rd, "Walking Bear"..$60.00 – 70.00 ea.

2nd Row:
1st, "Roll Over Cat" w/Box .$100.00 – 125.00
2nd, "Playful Cat" w/Box.......$75.00 – 100.00
3rd – 5th, Walking Bears ..$40.00 – 50.00 ea.

3rd Row:
"X Car," Lady Driver
    w/Box ....$125.00 – 150.00

"Walking Goat" w/Box ......$75.00 – 90.00
"Baby Tortoise" w/Box......$60.00 – 75.00

4th Row:
"Circus Elephant" w/Box .$200.00 – 225.00
"Elephant on Barrel"
    w/Box ....$400.00 – 450.00

5th Row:
"Dancing Couple" ....$40.00 – 50.00
Smaller Dancing Couple
    w/Box ....$50.00 – 60.00
"Jumping Dog" w/Box.......$40.00 – 50.00

Page 219
Top Row:
"Hopping Dog" w/Box.......$40.00 – 50.00
"Cowboy w/Two Guns"
    w/Box ....$100.00 – 125.00
Celluloid "Toddling Babe"
    w/Box ....$100.00 – 125.00

2nd Row:
"Playing Dog" w/Box ....$75.00 – 90.00
"Monkey Sweet Melodian"
    w/Box ....$100.00 – 125.00
Celluloid Swan w/Box.......$65.00 – 75.00
"Auto Cycle" w/Box ......$400.00 – 500.00

3rd Row:
"Sparkling Loop Plane"
    w/Box ....$250.00 – 300.00
"Penguin" w/Box ....$60.00 – 65.00
"Remote Control Car"
    w/Box ....$200.00 – 225.00

4th Row:
"Camel" w/Box.............$125.00 – 150.00
Small Car.........................$20.00 – 25.00
Celluloid "Cheery Cook"
    w/Box ....$100.00 – 125.00
Celluloid Boy "Circus Tricycle"
    w/Box ....$200.00 – 225.00

5th Row:
1st, Inflatable Football ......$20.00 – 22.50
2nd and 3rd, Inflatable Rabbits.$15.00 – 20.00 ea.

Page 220
Top Row:
"Angora Rabbit," three colors
    w/Box ....$35.00 – 40.00 ea.

2nd Row:
Hopping Squirrel w/Box .$75.00 – 100.00
"Jumping Rabbit" w/Box ...$75.00 – 80.00

3rd Row:
1st and 2nd, "Studebaker"
    w/Box ....$90.00 – 100.00 ea.
3rd, "Baby Pontiac" w/Box ..$65.00 – 75.00
4th, "Chevrolet with Back Motion"
    w/Box ....$100.00 – 125.00

4th Row:
"Sarcas" Celluloid Elephant
    w/Box ....$350.00 – 400.00
"Circus Elephant" w/Box .$325.00 – 375.00
"Sarcas" Celluloid Monkey
    w/Box ....$350.00 – 400.00

5th Row:
Celluloid "Cowboy" w/Box..$90.00 – 110.00
"Trick Seal" w/Celluloid Ball..$50.00 – 65.00
Celluloid Pink Seal w/Box .$90.00 – 100.00

Page 221
Top Row:
"Playful Little Dog" w/box .$75.00 – 85.00
"Hurricane Racer" w/box .$200.00 – 225.00
"Champion" w/box ....$100.00 – 125.00

2nd Row:
"Singing Canary" w/box ....$75.00 – 85.00
"Walking Bear" w/box ....$75.00 – 85.00
Penguin ....$30.00 – 40.00
"My Favorite Watch".........$10.00 – 15.00

3rd Row:
"Stem Winding Watch" ....$3.00 – 4.00 ea.
"Ice Cream Vendor" w/box .$150.00 – 175.00
Bamboo Snake, 15½".........$20.00 – 22.50
Rabbit.................................$18.00 – 20.00
"Hula" dancer (white).........$50.00 – 60.00
"Hula" dancer (black)
    w/box ....$100.00 – 125.00

4th Row:
"Ruby" Watch ....$6.00 – 7.50
"Special" Cigar ....$8.00 – 10.00 ea.
Tool Set.............................$60.00 – 75.00
Dog ....$18.00 – 20.00

Page 222
Top Row:
Village (10 Pieces)............$30.00 – 35.00
Football Player.................$10.00 – 12.00

2nd Row:
Cars in Original Boxes..$100.00 – 125.00 ea.
Wooden Puzzle ....$10.00 – 12.50
Rubber Knife ....$7.50 – 10.00

3rd Row:
Football ....$17.50 – 20.00
Checkers ....$12.50 – 15.00
Razzers...............................$5.00 – 6.00 ea.

Page 223
Top Row:
Monkey on Tricycle ....$75.00 – 100.00
Monkey ....$50.00 – 75.00
Celluloid Baseball Catcher.$100.00 – 125.00
Metal Dog ....$40.00 – 50.00
Celluloid Clown Monkey ..$80.00 – 100.00
Celluloid Xylophone Player .$100.00 – 125.00

2nd Row:
Celluloid Rabbit.............$100.00 – 125.00

Walking Camel ....$45.00 – 55.00
Walking Metal Duck..........$30.00 – 35.00
Flipping Celluloid Clown....$75.00 – 90.00

3rd Row:
Metal Tricycle, missing rider ..$15.00 – 17.50
Celluloid Boy w/Metal Case ..$75.00 – 90.00
Wind-up Car, 5" ....$50.00 – 60.00
Celluloid Flipping Monkey .$65.00 – 75.00
Wind-up Car, 3" ....$30.00 – 35.00

4th Row:
Hopping "Rudolph" Reindeer .$60.00 – 75.00
Celluloid Walking Santa..$400.00 – 450.00
Roller Skating Bear ......$200.00 – 225.00
Walking, Hopping Giraffe..$50.00 – 60.00
Celluloid Acrobatic
    Gymnast ....$125.00 – 150.00

5th Row:
Walking Lion ....$40.00 – 50.00
Hopping Dog w/Bone........$40.00 – 50.00
Walking Elephant..............$40.00 – 50.00
Walking Dog ....$30.00 – 35.00

Page 224
Top Row:
Horn ....$25.00 – 30.00
Alligator Clickers ....$40.00 – 45.00 dz.
Composition Doll...............$35.00 – 40.00
Silver-haired Doll ....$22.50 – 25.00
Microscope......................$85.00 – 100.00
Beetle Clicker in front of box ..$5.00 – 6.00

2nd Row:
Dionne Quints.................$85.00 – 100.00
Celluloid Monkey Car Mirror
    Hanger ....$22.50 – 25.00
Celluloid Monkey Car Mirror
    Hanger ....$12.50 – 15.00
Box of Eight Bisque Dolls ..$100.00 – 125.00

3rd Row:
1st and 2nd, Cameras ....$10.00 – 12.50 ea.
3rd, Mouse ....$7.50 – 10.00
4th, Rabbit, hanging ....$7.50 – 10.00
5th, Harmonica.................$17.50 – 20.00
6th, Harmonica ....$15.00 – 17.50
7th, Harmonica ....$15.00 – 17.50
8th and 9th, Compasses ....$17.50 – 20.00 ea.

4th Row:
"Special Police" Badge .....$12.50 – 15.00
Piano Baby ....$90.00 – 100.00
"Meyi Grand" on top..........$65.00 – 75.00
Mirror..............................$7.50 – 10.00
Pistol ....$12.50 – 15.00
Ukulele ....$40.00 – 50.00
Water Pistol, bird embossed on
    side....................................$6.00 – 8.00

5th Row:
Badminton Shuttlecock ....$8.00 – 10.00
Doll in Basket....................$30.00 – 35.00

Black Doll ....$45.00 – 50.00
Pair Black Dolls ....$60.00 – 75.00
Baby ....$30.00 – 35.00
Ping Pong Ball..................$12.50 – 15.00
Small Composition Doll......$22.50 – 25.00
Snow Baby w/Seal ....$35.00 – 40.00

Page 225
Top Row:
Vase, 3¾", embossed yellow
    rose ....$17.50 – 20.00
Vase, 3⅜", blue floral.........$17.50 – 20.00
Vase, 5⅞", blue w/gold
    handles ....$22.50 – 25.00
Vase, pink w/embossed blue
    rose ....$20.00 – 22.50
Vase, 6", urn style.............$20.00 – 22.50
Vase, 6¼", urn style..........$22.50 – 25.00
Vase, white blossoms ....$12.50 – 15.00
Vase, green with flowers......$8.00 – 10.00
Vase, green with floral scene..$8.00 – 10.00
Vase, yellow and blue stripe .$12.50 – 15.00
Vase, green w/embossed red
    rose ....$25.00 – 30.00

2nd Row:
1st and 2nd, Vases, 4¼", green
    w/embossed rose ....$15.00 – 17.50 ea.
3rd, 4th, and 8th, Vases, green, blue, or
    white w/embossed flowers .$7.50 – 10.00 ea.
5th and 6th, Vases, yellow w/embossed
    flowers ....$10.00 – 12.50 ea.
7th, Vase, rose w/lace ....$15.00 – 17.50
9th, Vase, pink w/white roses.$7.50 – 10.00
10th – 13th, Vases, orange or white
    w/flowers ....$4.00 – 5.00 ea.

3rd Row:
1st and 2nd, Vases, "Wedgwood-
    like"............................$7.50 – 10.00 ea.
3rd, Vase, 1¾", pink, fluted top.$5.00 – 6.00
4th and 11th, Vases, 2", white .$2.00 – 3.00 ea.
5th, Vase, 1⅞", gold handles .$3.00 – 4.00
6th, Vase, pink w/embossed
    flowers ....$5.00 – 6.00
7th, Vase, brown w/roses ......$4.00 – 5.00
8th, Vase, 3½" ....$12.50 – 15.00
9th and 10th, Vases............$7.50 – 10.00 ea.
12th Vase, green w/white spots.$8.00 – 10.00
13th and 14th, Vases, 3⅝".$10.00 – 12.50 ea.

4th Row:
1st, 9th, and 10th, Vases,
    4¼"..............................$12.50 – 15.00 ea.
2nd, Vase, 4¼" ....$12.50 – 15.00
3rd and 5th, Vases, white
    floral ....$5.00 – 6.00 ea.
4th, Vase ....$2.00 – 3.00
6th, Vase, two handled floral..$4.00 – 5.00
7th, Vase, pear shaped......$12.50 – 15.00
8th, Vase, garden scene ....$10.00 – 12.50
11th, Vase, Iris.................$12.50 – 15.00

5th Row:
1st, Vase, 3½", orange flower..$10.00 – 12.50

2nd, Vase, 3⅝", berries .....$10.00 – 12.50
3rd, Vase, pink corn ....$15.00 – 17.50
4th, Vase, floral ....$10.00 – 12.50
5th, Vase, blue w/red tulip .$10.00 – 12.50
6th, Vase, cornucopia ....$10.00 – 12.50
7th, Vase, pagoda scene ...$15.00 – 17.50
8th and 9th, Vases, embossed
    dragons ....$12.50 – 15.00 ea.
10th, Vase, green w/flowers ..$7.50 – 10.00
11th, Vase, carriage scene ....$6.00 – 8.00

Page 226
Top Row (Left to Right):
All Vases, Save 5th and 6th..$4.00 – 6.00 ea.
5th Vase, looks like Egyptian
    Hieroglyphics...................$8.00 – 10.00
6th, Kutani-type ....$6.00 – 8.00

2nd Row:
All Save 4th Pair ....$8.00 – 10.00 pr.
4th Pair, Kutani-type ....$16.00 – 20.00 pr.

3rd Row:
Six Kutani-types ....$8.00 – 10.00 ea.
2nd Vase (unusual shape) ....$8.00 – 10.00
6th, 7th, 8th Vases ....$5.00 – 6.00 ea.

4th Row:
Six Kutani-types ....$8.00 – 10.00 ea.
Others ....$3.00 – 4.00 ea.

Bottom:
All Vases.............................$3.00 – 5.00 ea.

Page 227
Top Row:
All Items ....$5.00 – 6.00

2nd Row:
All Items Save Topless Girl .$5.00 – 7.00
Topless Girl......................$10.00 – 12.00

3rd Row:
All Items Save Naked Girl and
    Wagon...........................$3.50 – 5.00
Naked Girl and Vase ....$12.00 – 15.00
Girl w/Wagon...................$12.00 – 15.00

4th Row:
All Items Save Angel on Star.$5.00 – 8.00
Angel on Shooting Star.....$10.00 – 12.00

5th Row:
All Items, Save Tree ....$8.00 – 10.00
Tree ....$4.00 – 5.00

Page 228
Top Row:
1st and 7th Vases ....$10.00 – 12.00 ea.
2nd, "Wedgwood" Vase ....$4.00 – 5.00
3rd, 4th, and 5th Vases
    (3½ – 4")...........................$6.00 – 8.00 ea.
6th Vase ....$12.50 – 15.00

Price Guide →

2nd Row:
1st and 6th Vase.................$8.00 – 10.00 ea.
2nd and 4th Vases.........$15.00 – 17.50 ea.
5th Vase.........................$25.00 – 30.00

3rd Row:
1st and 5th ....$25.00 – 30.00 pr.
2nd, 3rd, 4th Vases ....$35.00 – 40.00 ea.

4th Row:
1st Vase ....$15.00 – 20.00
2nd Vase ....$15.00 – 20.00
Dragon Vase ....$75.00 – 100.00

Page 229

Top Row:
Vase w/Floral Decoration, 8" ..$40.00 – 45.00
Same as 1st, except 6"......$30.00 – 35.00
Cornucopia....................$12.50 – 15.00
Pottery Vase...................$17.50 – 20.00
Raised Rose Bud Vase .....$15.00 – 18.00
Cylinder Vase, 8"............$30.00 – 35.00

2nd Row:
1st, Floral Two-handled, 4⅞" .$8.00 – 10.00
2nd, Rust Floral ....$8.00 – 10.00
3rd and 4th, Cornucopias w/Floral
   Design ....$6.00 – 8.00 ea.
5th, Two-handled Floral ....$6.00 – 8.00
6th, Pottery Decorated......$15.00 – 17.50
7th, Orange Floral ....$8.00 – 10.00
8th, Blue Floral ....$10.00 – 12.00

3rd Row:
1st, Floral, 2⅝"....................$2.00 – 3.00
2nd, Tulip ....$3.00 – 4.00
3rd, Blue Open Handled........$4.00 – 5.00
4th – 8th, Mini Vases ....$2.00 – 3.00 ea.
9th, Windmill Design...........$6.00 – 8.00
10th, Floral.......................$3.00 – 4.00
11th, Spatter Ware ....$6.00 – 8.00
12th, Embossed Children, 3" ..$10.00 – 12.00

4th Row:
Green Floral, 3⅞" ....$10.00 – 12.00
Blue w/Pink Flower............$8.00 – 10.00
Orange Flower.................$10.00 – 12.00
Footed Vase ....$6.00 – 8.00
Mexican Siesta ....$10.00 – 12.50
6th – 9th, Brown Vases ....$4.00 – 5.00 ea.

5th Row:
1st – 7th, Brown Vases, 3¾" to
   4"..............................$6.00 – 8.00 ea.
8th and 9th, Brown Vases .....$4.00 – 5.00 ea.

Page 230

Top Row:
All Vases.........................$8.00 – 10.00 ea.

2nd Row:
All Vases Save 2nd and 5th ..$8.00 – 10.00 ea.
2nd Vase, Children ....$10.00 – 12.00
5th Vase, Seated Figure....$20.00 – 25.00

3rd Row:
All Vases Save George
   Washington.....................$8.00 – 10.00
George Washington...........$12.00 – 15.00

Bottom:
1st Vase, fine quality..........$30.00 – 35.00
Iris Vases ....$60.00 – 75.00 ea.
4th Vase, enclosed figure ...$30.00 – 40.00
5th Vase ....$15.00 – 18.00

Page 231

Top Row:
Girl w/Apron, 4⅞" ....$10.00 – 12.50
Same, only 3⅞" ....$8.00 – 10.00
Chinese Boy in Vase, 6⅛" .$35.00 – 40.00
Colonial Lady in Vase ....$35.00 – 40.00
Two-handled Child Vase....$20.00 – 25.00
Colonial Man, 3¼"..............$5.00 – 6.00
Child w/Basket ....$8.00 – 10.00

2nd Row:
Oriental Lady, 4½" ....$15.00 – 18.00
Oriental Lady....................$20.00 – 25.00
Cowboy w/Cactus ....$12.50 – 15.00
Boy w/Accordion..................$5.00 – 6.00
"Hummel"-type Boy w/Violin.$15.00 – 17.50
Girl................................$10.00 – 12.00

3rd Row:
Colonial Girl, 2½"..................$3.00 – 4.00
Clown w/Egg ....$12.50 – 15.00
Brown Vase..........................$4.00 – 5.00
Boy w/Cart ....$5.00 – 6.00
Colonial by Flower...............$5.00 – 6.00
Mexican by Cactus...............$5.00 – 6.00
7th and 8th, Colonials...........$5.00 – 6.00 ea.

4th Row:
1st and 2nd, Colonial Lady or Man,
   3½"..............................$8.00 – 10.00 ea.
3rd, Vase w/Dancer..........$10.00 – 12.00
4th, Child.............................$4.00 – 5.00
5th, Lady w/Blue Basket ......$4.00 – 5.00
6th, Pottery-like Vase ....$6.00 – 8.00
7th – 9th, Lady or Man, 2"....$3.00 – 4.00 ea.

5th Row:
1st, Brown Vase, 2½"..........$8.00 – 10.00
2nd, Orange Vase, 2½".......$8.00 – 10.00
3rd – 5th, Oriental Vases,
   2½"..............................$8.00 – 10.00 ea.
6th, Oriental ....$10.00 – 12.00
7th and 8th, Oriental, 2½".....$6.00 – 8.00 ea.

Page 232

Top Row:
Brown, 4¼" ....$6.00 – 8.00
White, 4¾" ....$15.00 – 17.50
Swan, 5" ....$10.00 – 12.50
Ballerina, 8¼" ....$50.00 – 60.00
Flowers in Relief, 10⅛" ....$50.00 – 60.00
Blue and White, 8¼" ....$12.50 – 15.00
Boy Ready for Picnic, 5"...$10.00 – 12.50

2nd Row:
Dragon in Relief, 2⅝" ....$8.00 – 10.00
Daffodil, 4" ....$8.00 – 10.00
Embossed Flower, 5½".......$8.00 – 10.00
4th and 5th, 2¼"................$4.00 – 5.00 ea.
Bisque, 4"........................$15.00 – 20.00
Bisque, 4"........................$15.00 – 20.00
Swan, 5" ....$10.00 – 12.50
9th, 2⅝" and Bird in Relief,
   4".............................$8.00 – 10.00 ea.
Dragon, 2½"........................$5.00 – 6.00

3rd Row:
Tulip, 2⅜".........................$5.00 – 6.00
2nd and 9th, 3⅝".................$5.00 – 6.00
Swan, 3¾".......................$10.00 – 12.50
"Wedgwood"-type, 6⅛"......$40.00 – 50.00
Oriental Man, 4¾".............$18.00 – 20.00
"Wedgwood"-type, 6⅝".......$40.00 – 50.00
Scenic, 3¾".....................$12.50 – 15.00
Floral, 4¼"........................$8.00 – 10.00

4th Row:
2¼", "Pico" ....$4.00 – 5.00
2nd, 3rd, and 9th, 2¼" to 2½".$2.00 – 3.00 ea.
4th, 6th, 10th, 3" and 2"........$4.00 – 5.00 ea.
5th, 3½", "Moriyama" ....$6.00 – 8.00
7th Elf, 2½" ....$7.00 – 8.00
8th Wall Pocket, 2½" ....$6.00 – 8.00
11th Floral, 3" ....$6.00 – 8.00
12th Seated Girl, 3½" ....$10.00 – 12.50

5th Row:
1st "Wedgwood"-type, 2¾"..$8.00 – 10.00
2nd and 11th, 3" and 2⅜"......$4.00 – 5.00
3rd Pagoda in Relief, 5¼".$20.00 – 25.00
4th, 7th, and 9th, 4½" to 4¾"..$12.50 – 15.00
5th Tulip, 4".....................$10.00 – 12.50
6th Green, 4".......................$6.00 – 8.00
8th Cat Faces, 5" ....$20.00 – 22.50
10th Floral, 3" ....$5.00 – 6.00

Page 233

Top: Box 14" x 22"..........$90.00 – 100.00
Center: 10" signed "Andrea"..$300.00 – 400.00
Bottom: Fly rod in box ....$75.00 – 80.00

Page 234

Mikky Phonograph 4½" x 5¾" long x 4" tall
   (metal tag on box) ......$200.00 – 250.00

Page 235

Top left: 78 Record .....$15.00 – 20.00 ea.
Top right: 78 Record Set in
   Box ....$100.00 – 125.00
Bottom: Boy, 9" Florence Ceramics
   "look-alike"..................$45.00 – 50.00
   Girl mate, 8¼" ....$45.00 – 50.00

Page 236

Top left: 10" Swan Bisque
   Planter ....$100.00 – 125.00
Top right: Kaleidoscope of "Three Little
   Pigs"........................... $20.00 – 25.00

Bottom left: Two-sided Game
    Puzzle ....$20.00 – 25.00
Bottom right: Elf on Praying
    Mantis ....$20.00 – 25.00

Page 237
Top Row:
1st, 3rd, 5th, Dragon Cup and
    Saucer ....$15.00 – 20.00
2nd, Dragon Creamer and Lid..$30.00 – 35.00
4th, Dragon Sugar and Lid .$30.00 – 35.00
6th, Dragon Teapot ....$75.00 – 90.00
18-Piece Dragon Set ....$225.00 – 270.00

2nd Row:
1st, Angel Nudes Powder Jar.$45.00 – 50.00
2nd, Compote, two-piece, signed
    "Andrea" .... $150.00 – 200.00
3rd, Chef Cooking Wall Lamp..$35.00 – 40.00

3rd Row:
1st, Sad Mug ....$25.00 – 30.00
2nd, Indian Chief Ash Tray ..$15.00 – 20.00
3rd, Indian Condiment Set..$35.00 – 40.00
4th, Dog ....$12.50 – 15.00
5th, Ram's Head Pitcher ...$15.00 – 17.50

4th Row:
1st, Multi floral Cup and Saucer $15.00 – 20.00
2nd, Lacquerware Cloverleaf Flower
    Arranger ....$70.00 – 80.00

3rd, Miniature Cup and Saucer.$6.00 – 8.00
4th, Floral Cup and Saucer.$8.00 – 10.00

5th Row:
1st, Kaleidoscope of "Three Little
    Pigs" ....$20.00 – 25.00
2nd, Two-sided Game Puzzle..$20.00 – 25.00
3rd, Anniversary Clock with Swinging
    Geisha Girl Pendulum..$100.00 – 125.00
4th, Knight two-piece Decanter.$75.00 – 100.00
5th, Inflatable Rabbit ....$15.00 – 20.00

Page 238
Top Row:
1st, Bisque Lady with Basket of Flowers,
    8" ....$45.00 – 50.00
2nd, Bisque Mate with Water Sprinkler,
    8" ....$45.00 – 50.00
3rd, Porcelain Gentleman in Fine Detail,
    12" ....$75.00 – 100.00
4th, Porcelain Matching Lady,
    12".............................$75.00 – 100.00
5th, Porcelain Matching Lady, 10"..$55.00 – 65.00
6th, Porcelain Gentleman in Fine Detail,
    10" ....$55.00 – 65.00

2nd Row:
1st, "Praying" Girl Vase ....$12.50 – 15.00
2nd, Violin Playing Boy Vase..$12.50 – 15.00
3rd, Oriental Man, 7"........$20.00 – 22.50
4th, Oriental Woman, 7"....$20.00 – 22.50
5th, Unimpressed Girl,.......$10.00 – 12.50

6th, Boy Showing Biceps to Girl.$10.00 – 12.50
7th, Girl with Dog.............$10.00 – 12.50
8th. Boy with Dog ....$10.00 – 12.50

3rd Row:
1st, Turban Boy ....$8.00 – 10.00
2nd, Turban Boy Playing
    Instrument......................$8.00 – 10.00
3rd, Angel Watching Child .$30.00 – 35.00
4th, American Children "Little
    Astrologer" ....$100.00 – 125.00
5th, Shelf Sitter Playing Banjo .$10.00 – 12.50
6th, Shelf Sitter Playing Flute ..$10.00 – 12.50

4th Row:
1st, Cello Player with Ruffled
    Dress............................$20.00 – 25.00
2nd, Man Playing Violin ....$10.00 – 12.50
3rd, Child Playing Mandolin.$12.50 – 15.00
4th, Ballerina with Crinoline Skirt and
    Outstretched Arms........$20.00 – 22.50
5th, Ballerina with Crinoline Skirt .$18.00 – 20.00
6th, Shelf Sitter ....$12.50 – 15.00

5th Row:
1st, Uncle Sam, 4½" ....$1.00 – 17.50
2nd, Girl with Wide Skirt.....$8.00 – 10.00
3rd, Doll with Jointed Arms and Legs,
    7"................................$35.00 – 40.00
4th, Celluloid Doll, 6".........$25.00 – 30.00
5th, Figurine with Tongue that Goes In and
    Out ....$30.00 – 35.00